Seattle on FILM

by Randy Hodgins & Steve McLellan

 PUNCHLINE PRODUCTIONS

Today Comedy...Tomorrow the World

Roll the Credits . . .

Front and back cover design by Whitney Design, Olympia, Washington

Editorial Assistance by Terry Winfield

Printed and bound in the United States by Gorham Printing, Rochester, Washington

Photo Credits:

Front cover photos of Elvis Presley, Vicki Tui, and Norman Taurog by Paul Thomas, Seattle Times, and of Tom Hanks by Tom Reese, Seattle Times.

Back cover photo by Jeff Showman

All other photos by John Farrand unless otherwise noted.

ISBN: 0-9648184-1-8
Library of Congress: 95-074746

Punchline Productions
P.O. Box 22
Olympia, Washington 98507
(360) 493-6614

Table of Contents

ACKNOWLEDGEMENTS

In the words of the noted philosophers, the Grateful Dead, "What a long strange trip it's been." A lot has happened in the two years since Jim Morrison appeared to us in a dream and told us to write a book about films shot on location in Seattle. While this book is mostly the product of many trips to the video store, many late evenings of watching and re-watching, and many trips to Seattle to verify locations (most of which, fortunately, were near coffee shops and pubs) we did get a lot of help along the way. Many thanks to Donna James of the Seattle Film and Video Office; Eugene Mazzola, local film pro without peer; Leslie Lytel and Kathy Sanders from the State Film and Video Office; Lydia Evans of the Seattle Times photo library; the Staff of the Museum of History and Industry; Tumwater Video, Video Corner, and Scarecrow Video for their collections; Patty's Eggnest for much needed sustenance on our Seattle trips; and countless friends, relatives, and co-workers who were cheerleaders and pretended to laugh at our jokes.

Our greatest thanks go to Tina, Alex and Phillip Hodgins and Deb, Daniel and Matthew McLellan for being willing to give us up every Sunday night at nine, and for letting us hog the computer.

INTRODUCTION

Not too long ago, a friend of ours exclaimed, "So you guys are writing a book about films made in Seattle. You mean like **Sleepless in Seattle**? No one's gonna read that — are you guys nuts?" So we got discouraged and quit. The end.

Not quite. However, we have wondered why a book on movies filmed in Seattle hasn't already been written by some enterprising film critic or scholar. After all, over 40 major motion pictures have been shot here, dating as far back as the 1930's.

The answer became obvious to us once we had finally seen a fair number of these pictures. Most of the movies shot in Seattle over the last 30 years are mediocre at best — often they are downright terrible. Only a handful are worth watching as "films." But we kept watching anyway, mostly because we aren't film critics or scholars. Nope, we planted ourselves in our recliners, remotes at the ready, because these films do offer a unique view of Seattle over the years. The city's changing architecture and culture are framed in these cinematic time portals, giving us an enduring reminder of who we were, where we've been, and how far we've come or fallen, depending on your perspective.

For example, long-time Seattleites will find it hard to watch a movie like 1965's **The Slender Thread**, without growing nostalgic for a time when Seattle was the Jet City rather than the Emerald City. On the other hand, **Singles** shows us a 1992 portrait of a metropolis that is vibrant, alive, and on the cutting edge of popular culture. Both cities still exist — especially in the neighborhoods — but many of the cultural landmarks preserved on film have fallen victim to time, economics, or indifference.

A Brief History of Seattle on Film

The first major motion picture to be shot on location in Seattle was **Tugboat Annie**, way back in 1933. However, there was a "minor" 30-year dry spell of Seattle pictures until Elvis Presley came to the 1962 World's Fair to shoot the cleverly titled **It Happened at the**

World's Fair. Thus, the real history of Seattle film begins in 1963 with the release of the King's thirteenth feature length film. Rumor has it that Elvis liked the fries at Dick's so much he still keeps a secret apartment in Wallingford.

During the 1970's the pace of moviemaking picked up considerably. Some of these films are considered minor classics, like **Cinderella Liberty** (1973), or have become cult favorites like **The Parallax View** (1974). Far more of the movies were standard production line potboilers, and Seattle had its own run of the "tough cops who play by their own rules" films that were popular at the time. Billy Dee Williams (**Hit**), John Wayne (**McQ**), and Connie Stevens (**Scorchy**) all took turns playing Dirty Harry or Harriet during the decade.

All of these early films tended to trumpet their Seattle location, as if to say "Gee, look at us. Our massive budget allowed us to shoot this picture somewhere other than Hollywood." By the early 1980s, the economic and physical attractiveness of Seattle as a movie location became better known, and the number of films shot in the city increased sharply. They also tended to be better films. A moodier, grittier side of the city emerged in films like **Trouble in Mind** (1985) and **House of Games** (1987), both of which used Seattle's wet climate as the backdrop for dark tales of intrigue and betrayal. Similarly, **Twice in a Lifetime** (1985), **Frances** (1982), and **Wargames** (1983) dealt with serious and often depressing subjects like divorce, mental illness, and nuclear holocaust.

For Seattle film fans, the early 1990's have produced a bumper crop. Through the middle of 1995, fifteen films either entirely or partially shot in Seattle have been released, with several more scheduled. If this pace continues, the current decade could surpass the total output of the 1970's and 1980's combined. So far, the 1990's have continued the moody tone set in the 1980's, though the blockbuster **Sleepless in Seattle** (1993) may reposition the city as a backdrop for light comedy and romance.

The Seattle Filmmaking Industry

Today, moviemaking is big business in Washington State. Filmmakers spent over $50 million in the state in 1994 and more than $300 million since 1981. While the bulk of the work is in television shows and commercials, the state's connection with major filmmakers is strong and growing. Current plans to turn part of the Sand Point Naval Air Station into a soundstage could fuel explosive growth in the state film industry. Contrast that with a $13 million annual economic impact a decade ago, and it is clear that, unlike commercial fishing and timber, movies are a growth industry in Washington.

But, why Seattle? There are a number of reasons. First, the state of Washington and the city of Seattle have established special offices to "troll" for filmmakers, and to make it easier for them to do business once they are here. This involves arranging for everything from street closures and parking, to finding locations for scenes, to negotiating with neighbors who are not pleased to find their neighborhoods invaded by trucks, lights, cameras, and hundreds of cast, crew, and gawking onlookers.

Donna James of the Seattle Film and Video Office says that her role often resembles that of a peace mediator, looking for creative solutions to nasty problems. When **Sleepless in Seattle** was filming, the production company rented a house for filming. That was fine, except for the neighbor who had planned his wedding and reception for the same day shooting was to begin. Eventually, the neighbor agreed to end his reception early, and the film company bussed him and all of his guests to the Sorrento Hotel for a catered party, and then rented him the honeymoon suite to boot. Of course, **Sleepless in Seattle** was a romance — what would have happened to the poor guy's reception if the filmmaker had been David Lynch? The possibilities are too frightening to list.

Filmmakers also prize Seattle for its cloudy light, which allows a great deal of flexibility and control. In 1973, Mark Rydell who directed **Cinderella Liberty**, told the Seattle Post-Intelligencer, "Overcast cuts the light and that gives you more realistic tones in the color. There has been a change in the level of acceptance of reality — you need the realistic location and the realistic tones." Twenty years later, famed filmmaker Bernardo Bertolucci told the local press that he came to Seattle to make **Little Buddha** because the cold Northwest light came through on film. Bertolucci also praised Seattle's skyline, and particularly its culture, lauding Seattle as a "little capital" that had a distinctive, cosmopolitan European spirit. Not exactly the kind of publicity that would please Emmett Watson's Lesser Seattle movement.

All of these factors point to a bright future for Seattle as a major film production site. But there we are, looping off into a dense discussion of film economics and sociology when there are real questions to be answered. Questions like "How many times does the Space Needle appear in Seattle films?" and "How did Meg Ryan manage to drive from Lake Union to Alki in **Sleepless in Seattle**, keeping her eye on Tom Hanks' boat all the way, and not drive into Elliott Bay?" For these and other answers, we have to turn to the movies themselves.

About the Movies

Since **It Happened at the World's Fair,** hundreds of movies, television shows, and commercials have been filmed in Washington. Our focus is narrower. We have searched only for **major** motion pictures that were filmed on location in Seattle. This leaves out many popular television movies like **The Night Strangler** (1972), made for cable features like **Third Degree Burn** (1989), big screen films like **An Officer and a Gentleman** (1982) that were filmed outside the Seattle area, and low-budget, independent releases like **Birthright** (1990). We also ignored films that purported to be set in Seattle, but that were shot somewhere else, like **Stakeout** (1987) and **Stay Tuned** (1992). You can't fool us — much.

As is obvious by now, neither of us is a professional film critic, so we won't try to deconstruct the movies, or comment on how the director used advanced visual techniques to build tension. That's for the John Hartls and William Arnolds of the world. Nope, we either like a film or don't and we can tell you two or three reasons why. So our reviews focus on the basic plot (though in the case of some of these movies that's stretching it), the key Seattle landmarks that are featured, and bloopers that locals will appreciate. Each movie gets a rating of one to four Space Needles. Movie quality doesn't count half as much as how well Seattle locations and references were used — although if a film is a world class stinker we'll tell you (see our review of **Bombs Away**).

So sit back, fluff-up your pillow, crack open a microbrew or froth up a latte and prepare to enjoy three decades of **Seattle on Film.**

Director Mark Rydell and the cast of the 1973 cult favorite **Cinderella Liberty** relax on the ferry Spokane. Background: Tiny Freeman; Producer-Director Mark Rydell. Foreground: Kirk Calloway, James Caan, Marsha Mason. **(Karen Engstrom/Seattle Times)**

sixties and seventies

A man and his ham. Governor Albert Rosellini presents Elvis with a ham fit for a King during filming of **It Happened at the World's Fair**. Elvis is reputed to have eaten the entire ham seconds after this photograph was taken. **(Seattle Post Intelligencer Collection, Museum of History and Industry.)**

IT HAPPENED AT THE WORLD'S FAIR (MGM-1963)

Cast:	ELVIS PRESLEY (Mike Edwards), JOAN O'BRIEN (Diane Warren), GARY LOCKWOOD (Danny Burke), VICKY TUI (Sue-Lin), EDITH ATWATER (Miss Steuben), GUY RAYMOND (Barney Thatcher), KAM TONG (Walter Ling), YVONNE CRAIG (Dorothy Johnson)
Director:	Norman Taurog
Producer:	Ted Richmond
Screenplay:	Si Rose and Seamon Jacobs
Music:	Leith Stevens
Length:	105 minutes
Released:	April 1963
Rating:	Not Rated

Precisely three decades after the release of **Tugboat Annie,** *Seattle finally bounced back to the silver screen. Thanks in part to the perseverance of Governor Albert D. Rosellini, who personally wrote to MGM promoting the idea of a movie featuring Elvis at the World's Fair, the Hollywood bigwigs decided to use the fair as the backdrop for the King's thirteenth feature length film. Essentially a cinematic postcard,* **It Happened at the World's Fair** *is a must for any amateur Seattle or Elvis film historian.*

Film Synopsis

As in many other "event" movies, filmmakers have lashed together the thinnest of plots in order to show off a big star at a big event. Elvis plays Mike Edwards, an itinerant crop duster who is a partner of a compulsive, but lovable gambler named Danny Burke (Gary Lockwood). The boys are spraying in the fictional Washington town of "Sherrington" when the gambling debts mount, and their plane is seized by the local sheriff. They hitchhike to Seattle in search of work, and along the way are picked up by a kindly Asian farmer and his "gosh, isn't she cute as a bug's ear" niece Sue-Lin (Vicki Tui). Turns out, Uncle Walter (Kam Tong) and Sue-Lin are headed for the World's Fair in Seattle, so the boys decide to tag along.

Once they reach Seattle, Uncle Walter is called away, leaving Elvis to squire little Sue-Lin around the World's Fair. Now, the hardened cynic in you might say, "Hey, isn't it a bit strange that this kindly farmer is leaving his little niece in the care of a vagrant, unemployed hitchhiker who he just met, without even arranging a time to meet?" But this is Seattle in the early sixties, before it became a real city.

After a monorail ride, Elvis and Sue-Lin do some grazing at all the classic junk food outlets. Soon the peanuts and cotton candy give Sue-Lin a tummyache and Elvis takes her to the dispensary where he meets the token "love interest," nurse Diane Warren (Joan O'Brien). Diane's major distinguishing feature is her gravity-defying bosom, a feature shared by most of the women in the film.

The remainder of the movie shifts back and forth between Elvis' attempts to (1) uncover the mystery of the gravity-defying bosom, (2) reunite Sue-Lin with Uncle Walter who somehow becomes lost on a produce run, and (3) foil an international fur smuggling ring. We could go on in intricate detail about all of the plot devices, subtexts, and literary references, but hey, this is an Elvis flick.

Of course, in an Elvis flick there are songs (except for the awful **Change of Habit**, but that will be covered in our next book, **Films that Elvis Must Account For with God**). Elvis strums a ukelele in the back of Uncle Walter's pickup truck, Elvis sings a lullaby to little Sue-Lin, and Elvis serenades nurse Warren in the Space Needle restaurant. In the film's most surreal scene, Elvis strolls around a mobile home park, strumming an acoustic guitar and getting those polyester-clad geezers just a tappin' their toes and bein' hip with that crazy music.

Unlike many of his later films, Elvis actually attempts to act in **It Happened at the World's Fair**. In one memorable scene, he turns up his nose at a belgian waffle, though perhaps only because it wasn't deep fried and smeared with peanut butter and bacon. In a deep philosophical moment — no doubt predicting the rise of the men's movement some 30 years later — Elvis notes that "some women think they can destroy you." Here is a man fully in touch with his "inner King."

Seattle People, Places and Things

Seattle is the real star of **It Happened at the World's Fair,** and a must-see for anyone who was at the World's Fair, or who is old enough to lie and say they were. The Fair's "Man in the Space Age" theme is in full view, and the relentlessly cheerful depiction of the future is enough to make you glad that predictions of the future are always wrong. There is one unforgivable omission — there is no shot of the Bubbleator. This grievous lack of a Bubbleator costs the film half-a-needle on our rating scale.

While the World's Fair is adequately covered, the rest of the city is almost completely ignored. In many scenes, the stars are superimposed on cheesey backdrop projections that are designed to give the audience the illusion that the scene was shot on location. Still, the Seattle footage they shot led to a few great bloopers. Early on in the film when the boys are riding in Uncle Walter's pickup truck, the stock background shots change from the San Bernardino Mountains in Southern California to a full view of Mount Rainier. If that wasn't enough, our most famous landmark then manages to pull off the impossible by appearing in front of and behind the truck within minutes. After an obligatory song with Sue-Lin, the truck passes under the old wooden trestle at SE 8th and 121st in Bellevue and immediately rounds the corner into downtown Seattle. Traffic must have been light across 520.

Another blooper of sorts is the soundtrack, containing such memorable Elvis gems as "Take Me to the Fair," "Cotton Candy Land," and "Happy Ending." Background vocals were provided by the Jordanaires and the Mello Men. The Mello Men? No word from RCA on when the digitally remastered "Best of the Mello Men" boxed set will be available.

What Others Said

*"It **Happened at the World's Fair** is something that shouldn't have happened at all. Elvis Presley's budding dramatic talents have been neatly nipped in the Seattle story, which emerges as a dismal parody of the MGM musicals of old."*

Eugene Archer, New York Times

"Elvis still seems to be having fun in this one, and you will too."

Mick Martin

Summary

Overall, **It Happened at the World's Fair** is a pleasant treat. Just the right film for a late evening alone, or a hung-over Sunday afternoon on the couch. Be sure to lay in lots of pork rinds, pizza rolls, and beer before you watch this one — the King would.

THE SLENDER THREAD
(Paramount-1965)

Cast:	SIDNEY POITIER (Alan Newell), ANNE BANCROFT (Inga Dyson), TELLY SAVALAS (Dr. Joe Coburn), STEVEN HILL (Mark Dyson), INDUS ARTHUR (Marion), DABNEY COLEMAN (Charlie), ED ASNER (Detective Judd Riley)
Director:	Sydney Pollack
Producer:	Stephen Alexander
Screenplay:	Stirling Silliphant
Music:	Quincy Jones
Length:	98 minutes
Released:	December 1965
Rating:	Not Rated

*In 1964, journalist Shana Alexander (yes, the same Shana Alexander of **60 Minutes** "Point-Counterpoint" fame), wrote a series of articles for Life magazine describing the psychological crisis that led a Seattle housewife to attempt suicide. Out of this came **The Slender Thread**, a film that dramatized the work of the Seattle Crisis Clinic. Filmed in black and white, the film marked the directorial debut of Sydney Pollack, and another tour-de-force performance from Sidney Poitier.*

Film Synopsis

Based on the sobering statistic that "every two minutes someone attempts suicide in the United States," **The Slender Thread** tells the story of Inga Dyson (Anne Bancroft), a woman who has taken an overdose of barbiturates, and the crisis clinic volunteer who takes her call for help. Sidney Poitier plays Alan Newell, a psychology student at the UW who is volunteering at the clinic one evening when the call comes in. When Inga tells him that she has taken an overdose of sleeping pills, he frantically tries to get some clues to her identity and location, recognizing that the telephone line has become the "slender thread" with which he must save her life.

In a long series of flashbacks that comprise the bulk of the film, Newell manages to learn the details of Inga's life that have led to her suicide attempt. Gradually, we learn that she is married to commerical fisherman Mark Dyson (Steven Hill), and that they have a teenaged son. Only recently, Mark has discovered that he is not the biological father and refuses to forgive his wife for deceiving him.

As the telephone company tries to trace the call, the police department pieces together some of the information that Newell has been able to wring out of Inga during their telephone conversation. With less than 30 minutes before the sleeping pills will take her life, the frantic chase to locate Inga intensifies. Finally, the phone company comes through and the call is traced to a motel near Sea-Tac airport on Pacific Highway South. Once inside her room, the police find her unconscious, but still breathing. Relieved, Newell lets forth with a shout of joy, and calmly returns to the phone to take the next call.

Seattle People, Places and Things

Although **The Slender Thread** was not a major box office hit, its use of mid-sixties Seattle locations deserves recognition. Essentially, the first ten minutes of the film is a Seattle "travelogue." Nary a word of dialogue is spoken as the camera pans over every major landmark in town, from the Seattle Center to downtown and back to the UW. Although by 1965 most Hollywood movies were shot routinely in color, **The Slender Thread** is a black and white offering, which gives the city a sharp-edged look and tends to reinforce the documentary mood of the picture.

During these opening scenes, we see student Sidney Poitier exit the Suzzallo library into a sun-drenched, grass-covered, "pre-Red Square." He climbs aboard his bicycle and pedals thru campus to his car. Once inside, he drives through the U-District and down Campus Parkway toward Terry and Lander Halls, before the construction of the Condon Hall Law School. The camera also focuses on Inga who is seen staring sadly into the fountain at the Pacific Science Center and then driving her station wagon across the Ballard Bridge. Mark Dyson is also shown in his fishing boat near the Ballard Locks.

Much of the picture is shot inside the offices of the crisis clinic where there are few visual clues of Seattle. Exterior shots of the clinic, however, place the location on the west side of Capitol Hill overlooking Eastlake, with views over I-5 towards the Seattle Center and Queen Anne Hill. The search for Inga also leads to her Ballard home at the westernmost end of 70th St. N.W. It is here that she attempts suicide for the first time by walking straight into the sound. Not an easy thing to do since the house sits up on a bluff, a couple hundred feet above the water.

Unlike many films which would come after it, **The Slender Thread** does an admirable job with its "local" references. In describing himself to Inga, Alan Newell mentions that he's "a student at the U." A copy of the Seattle Post-Intelligencer in Inga's hotel room bears the date of June 12, 1965, right at the end of spring quarter, which ties to an earlier reference by Alan that he is studying for final exams. Later, when police detective Judd Riley (Ed Asner) thinks about running a license check on Inga's car, he bemoans the fact that "it'll take an hour to get an answer from Olympia." Only an hour? Boy, this was a long time ago. The only real "blooper" in the movie is an inadvertent reference to "King's County Hospital," a mispronouncement of the earlier name for Harborview Medical Center.

The music in the film is also a plus. The jazz-oriented score was arranged and composed by Seattle's own Quincy Jones. In one flashback, Inga and Mark are seen at a local discotheque listening to the "happening" sounds of a local rock and roll group (referred to in the credits as the "Sons of Adam"), and boogeying in a pre-grunge mosh pit. Do you suppose Pearl Jam was watching? Do you suppose they were born?

What Others Said

"Pollack allows or encourages Poitier to wave his arms like a windmill trying to dodge Sancho Panza, and allows or encourages Miss Bancroft to luxuriate in the bathos of Stirling Silliphant's dialogue."

Newsweek

"Poitier does ample justice, in a wonderfully restrained style, to an exacting assignment." "Miss Bancroft's performance is tender, knowing, graduated in intensity and convincing."

A.H. Weiler, New York Times

Summary

Although not generally available in video stores, **The Slender Thread** occasionally pops-up on television, most often on cable's American Movie Classics. The film is basically a tribute to Seattle's pioneering Crisis Clinic and suicide hotline, and that alone should place the picture in the Seattle on Film Hall of Fame (if there was one). Generally inspired performances from the lead actors and the somewhat unusual black and white views of the city, firmly establish **The Slender Thread** as a **Seattle on Film** classic.

Inga Dyson's house still stands overlooking the Shilshole Marina at the far end of 70th St. NW. The black and white film made the setting appear moodier than it does in person. (Private residence, please do not disturb.)

HARRY IN YOUR POCKET
(United Artists-1973)

Cast:	JAMES COBURN (Harry), MICHAEL SARRAZIN (Ray), TRISH VAN DEVERE (Sandy), WALTER PIDGEON (Casey), MICHAEL C. GWYNNE (Fence), TONY GIORGIO (First Detective), MICHAEL STEARNS (Second Detective)
Director:	Bruce Geller
Producer:	Bruce Geller
Screenplay:	James David Buchanan and Ronald Austin
Music:	Lalo Schifrin
Length:	103 minutes
Released:	August 1973
Rating:	PG (sexual situations, language)

*While two major motion pictures in 10 years was more than many cities could boast, by the early 1970's, Seattle clearly wanted more. While **It Happened at the World's Fair** and **The Slender Thread** were proud achievements, they were not really the product of any organized effort to promote the city as a major film destination. In 1972, Mayor Wes Uhlman went to work promoting Seattle as a viable Hollywood alternative with the creation of the Film Advisory Committee within the old Office of Economic Development. The campaign worked, and **Harry in Your Pocket** became the first major motion picture to be shot primarily in Seattle in the 1970's.*

Film Synopsis

As the film opens, we meet Ray (Michael Sarrazin), a lead-fingered pickpocket plying his trade in Seattle's King Street Station. Soon, he is caught by Sandy (Trish Van Devere) in the act of lifting her watch, but rather than turn him in, she befriends and goes to bed with him (this was a different time after all). His fence, disgusted with Ray's penny-ante merchandise, connects him with Casey (Walter Pidgeon), who is the main operative for Harry (James Coburn) a master pickpocket. After an initial meeting, Casey introduces Ray and Sandy to Harry, who agrees to bring them into his operation.

What follows is a fascinating look into the world of professional pickpockets. The scam seems simple enough. Casey is the "steer" who identifies promising marks and guides them in Harry's direction. Sandy is the "stall" who distracts the "mark" while Harry lifts their wallet. Harry then immediately hands off the "poke" to Ray who then passes it back to Casey to "skin." Harry's main rule — pounded into your head again and again — is that "Harry never holds." As a result, Harry has never been caught. Harry also has other rules, the most significant being no drug use and little alcohol use, though in almost every scene Harry is drinking copious quantities of stiff bourbon. It makes one wonder what "a lot" of alcohol use would be.

The gang continues to practice their pickpocket drills on the streets of Seattle with varying degrees of ineptitude. Back at the hotel, Harry's wandering eye turns to Sandy which begins to drive a wedge between her and Ray. That tension is put on hold, however, as the Seattle police — ever vigilant — learn Harry is in town and pay a visit to his hotel room. Harry decides that greener pastures are called for and the whole mob hops the ferry to Victoria. While the remainder of the movie is not filmed in Seattle, it contains the best footage of smoothly executed pickpocket routines.

Seattle People, Places and Things

Only the first half of the movie is shot in Seattle, but it is well worth the rental to see the pre-Kingdome city. After an opening shot at Sea-Tac airport, the action moves to the King Street Station. In the background you can hear the station master announcing Amtrak connections to "Tacoma, East Olympia, Centralia, Kelso, Vancouver and Portland . . . ."

The action then moves to the waterfront, where Sandy and Ray sit at some tables outside on the deck at Pier 57. There are also some good shots of the backside of a pre-renovation Pike Place Market as Ray and Sandy walk past the Oceanic Building, and other areas between the waterfront and First Avenue (remember the old white wooden staircase which led down to the waterfront from First and Union?). The pre-Four Seasons Olympic Hotel is also prominently featured, where Harry is camped out in room 3960.

Much of the Seattle footage was shot in Pioneer Square. Now, remember the time — circa 1972 and 1973. Pioneer Square had just undergone a major renovation and was the showplace of the city. You could have dinner at the trendy Brasserie Pittsbourg (which Casey, Ray, and Sandy did), and then walk in the sunshine without stepping over more than a half dozen winos. In the background, the Smith Tower looms magnificently before it was overshadowed by the 1980's building boom. While other Seattle shots include a nice sequence on the monorail, 34 minutes into the film comes the feature cameo — Mayor Wesley Uhlman himself becomes a victim of Harry's pickpocket gang as he leaves a Seattle First National Bank branch.

What Others Said

"*Harry in Your Pocket* *is a film with good performances, eye-catching settings (thanks for noticing), absorbing story —— and achieves every one of them with clean precision.*"

Lawrence Van Gelder, New York Times

The picture is "an engaging story of a group of super-pickpockets and how they prey upon innocent victims. Pidgeon steals the film as a sleazy professional crook."

Leonard Maltin

Summary

One of the movies filmed during the life of the first Seattle film office, **Harry in Your Pocket** is a mildly enjoyable caper. While not a great film, the picture offers enough location shots and one great cameo to be worth a trip to the video store.

CINDERELLA LIBERTY
(20th Century Fox-1973)

Cast:	JAMES CAAN (John Baggs, Jr.), MARSHA MASON (Maggie Paul), KIRK CALLOWAY (Doug), ELI WALLACH (Forshay), BURT YOUNG (Master at Arms), BRUCE KIRBY, JR. (Alcott), DABNEY COLEMAN (Executive Officer)
Director:	Mark Rydell
Producer:	Mark Rydell
Screenplay:	Darryl Poniscan
Music:	John Williams
Length:	117 minutes
Released:	December 1973
Rated:	R (language, nudity)

While many critics were unkind to **Cinderella Liberty** *on its release, it is a must for* **Seattle on Film** *fans for its generous view of the seedy side of the city in the early 1970's.* **Cinderella Liberty** *was the beginning of the first real renaissance of Seattle as a film location and, with* **McQ**, *presents a city that is far from a yuppie paradise.*

Film Synopsis

John Baggs, Jr. (James Caan) is a sailor who lands in the Seattle Navy Hospital. He is granted leave that ends at midnight — known as "Cinderella Liberty" — and promptly heads to the bars on First Avenue for some fun.

At the Club Neptune, Baggs is taken with a tough, but pretty pool hustler named Maggie Paul (Marsha Mason). He lets her take him a few games, then ups the ante — his fifty dollars against a roll in the hay. Naturally he wins, and they go to her seedy apartment for the payoff. There he learns that Maggie is mother to Doug (Kirk Calloway), a moody, malnourished street kid, who endures life on the couch while mom makes a living in the bedroom. Baggs falls for Maggie, and becomes a surrogate father to Doug. The bulk of the movie is a relationship study, with the untrusting Doug slowly learning to open up to Baggs, while Maggie continually sabotages her chance at a better life.

During his stay at the base, Baggs meets Forshay (Eli Wallach), a miserable former commander who is now being drummed out of the military. Later Baggs runs into Forshay in his new job, as a barker at one of downtown's seedier strip joints. The scene gives Baggs a chance to reflect on his desire to build a real life and family outside the military, and it gives Eli Wallach a chance to demonstrate some Oscar-caliber overacting.

While their relationship has many twists, ultimately Maggie rabbits on Baggs, sticking him with Doug. Living up to his image as the sensitive swabbie, Baggs promises to meet Doug on the docks the next morning and take him to New Orleans, where Maggie has fled with a young sailor. The next morning Doug -- now trusting in Baggs -- frantically searches the crowded docks to no avail. If this were a moody European film, it would end here, but a happier ending is needed for Americans (see **The Vanishing** for another example), and one is shortly forthcoming. We won't give away the nice twist at the end, but all's reasonably well that ends reasonably well.

Seattle People, Places and Things

Cinderella Liberty is a feast for fans of early 1970's Seattle. The film opens with a glorious shot of the Space Needle and Elliott Bay, panning across a skyline that is dominated by the Smith Tower. We next see a lingering view of the old Public Health Hospital looming over the city from its perch on Beacon Hill.

From there we head to First Avenue — and not the First Avenue of precious gelato stands, antique dealers and clothing merchants. This First Avenue sells nothing but booze and porn. Olympia Beer window signs alternate with marquees advertising "Books, Magazines, and Plastic Novelties." Somehow we don't think they mean little Space Needle replicas. This homey neighborhood also hosts Maggie's apartment, labeled the "Weston Apts" which were located just down the stairwell of the Grand Pacific Building on First and Seneca. Unfortunately, the Club Neptune, which hosts much of the action, was constructed by the filmmakers, though we did visit every bar we could find in search of the inspiration.

Cinderella Liberty includes a gratuitous ferry ride, as well as generous helpings of the ferry terminal, the old Greyhound bus station, and the Alaskan Way viaduct. But most of all it features the seamy, seedy and very alive heart of the old city. It also has a moment that could only have happened on First Avenue. Early in the film, as Baggs and Maggie make their way out of the Club Neptune, they are approached by a panhandler on the street. The scene was unplanned — the panhandler simply stumbled into the shot, taking Caan for a real sailor. While Marsha Mason is visibly flustered, Caan manages to stay completely in character and gives up some spare change. The filmmakers had to chase the panhandler down the street to get him to sign a release, and they fortunately had the sense to leave this priceless moment in the film.

There are also a few cultural markers that date the film. Metro busses appear frequently, painted in a vibrant red. On one bus is an advertisement for KIRO-FM, when it played 24-hour Mantovani and used the slogan "The difference is the music." The film also visits the Seattle Center Fun Forest, when the hottest ride in town was the Wild Mouse, and Gasworks Park before it became "urbanly renewed."

While moviemaking has now become common in Seattle, at the time, **Cinderella Liberty** was a big deal. In a 1973 Seattle P-I article, director Mark Rydell said, "The look of the city was perfect," pointing out that it had a "slightly nautical flavor," varied with skyscrapers, open-air markets on the piers, sleazy honky-tonk section and plenty of ships. While our overcast skies set the mood, they also helped with the filming. "Overcast cuts the light," Rydell explained when he was filming in Seattle, "and that gives you more realistic tones in the color." Rydell's comments would be echoed two decades later by Bernardo Bertolucci as he filmed **Little Buddha**, though he referred to the city as "delightfully European." Europe must have more seedy dives than we thought.

What Others Said

"Mark Rydell's films are nothing if not commercial and **Cinderella Liberty** *isn't commercial. Rydell has one foot in forties movies and the other in a Gucci; neither is on the ground."*

Pauline Kael

The film "is a nicely acted but aggressively false and sentimental comedy . . . almost everything that happens in the film is unbelievable, designed for short-term audience effect or easy laughter or tears."

Vincent Canby, New York Times

Summary

Cinderella Liberty has achieved an improved reputation over time, and is worth a rental simply to revel in the glories of a Seattle that used to be. Real nostalgists will want to view this one with **McQ** and **Scorchy** for a Seattle seventies triple-treat.

Looking a bit more "urbanly renewed" than in 1973, the doorway to Marsha Mason's seedy apartment building can be found down the stairwell outside the Grand Pacific Building at First and Seneca.

McQ
(Warner Brothers-1974)

Cast:	JOHN WAYNE (Lon McQ), EDDIE ALBERT (Captain Kosterman), DIANA MULDAUR (Lois Boyle), CLU GULAGER (Frank Toms), COLLEEN DEWHURST (Myra), JIM WATKINS (J.C.), DAVID HUDDLESTON (Pinky), AL LETTIERI (Santiago), ROGER E. MOSLEY (Rosey)
Director:	John Sturges
Producer:	Jules Levy and Arthur Gardner
Screenplay:	Lawrence Roman
Music:	Elmer Bernstein
Length:	116 minutes
Released:	February 1974
Rating:	PG (violence and language)

The idea of John Wayne as a "tough cop" was not all that shocking considering the popularity of the genre in the early seventies. Films like **Dirty Harry, Serpico,** *and* **The French Connection,** *all celebrated the "tough cop who plays by his own rules" and all were big hits at the box office. What was surprising was that after more than four decades of war movies and westerns, the "Duke" had never before played the role of a cop or private eye.*

Film Synopsis

John Wayne plays police lieutenant Lon McQ (we never learn the full surname), a crusty veteran of the Seattle Police Department whose world-weary cynicism is matched only by his loose regard for civil liberties. The story revolves around McQ's investigation of the murder of his partner and closest friend on the force. When his efforts are impeded by the police bureaucracy ("damn politics" he charges), McQ resigns from the force. Unknown to Lon at the time, but revealed to the audience, his partner is shown to have been a killer himself, and part of a local drug trafficking ring. Although McQ's boss Captain Kosterman (Eddie Albert) blames "radicals and terrorists" for the murders, McQ believes that a local drug kingpin named Santiago (Al Lettieri) is behind the trouble.

Proving that Dirty Harry has nothing on him, McQ corners Santiago in a local restaurant lavatory and proceeds to trample the legal niceties that leave criminals on the loose. As Santiago lays sprawled out on the floor, his face bloodied by McQ's fists, his henchmen arrive. McQ simply chortles that "he must have slipped on the floor and fell." Unhappy about not being assigned to the case, McQ continues his own investigation as a private detective. He encounters other characters like Myra (Colleen Dewhurst), a lonely cocaine-addicted cocktail waitress and Rosey (Roger E. Moseley), a black, street-wise hustler (see Antonio Vargas as "Huggy Bear"), who first tells him that his dead partner was a crook.

Throughout the film Lois Boyle (Diana Muldaur), the wife of McQ's dead partner, fools him with her displays of grief and desire to "run away" to Canada. In reality, she's in cahoots with another dirty cop named Frank Toms (Clu Gulager), and they conspire to frame McQ for the drug trade. When Captain Kosterman's internal affairs investigation closes in, McQ kidnaps Lois and the drugs, and heads for the coast. After a thrilling chase scene on the beach at Moclips between McQ and Santiago's gang (who have shown up to try and steal back the real drugs), a gun battle ensues and McQ wipes out the small band with the help of his trusty semi-automatic (these were the days when the police were better armed than the crooks). As Kosterman and the other police arrive and realize McQ's innocence, they implore him to rejoin the force. Resigned to returning to the only life he knows, Wayne mutters "let's get a drink" and the film ends.

Seattle People, Places and Things

From the opening scene of the Seattle waterfront at dawn, which provides the background for the cold blooded murder of two police officers and a drug trafficking police detective, **McQ** telegraphs that this is a dark, dirty and foreboding Seattle, a far cry from the future "most liveable city in America." This is Seattle before gentrification, before baseball moved indoors and before the Pike Place Market became a place to browse instead of shop.

Much of the action in **McQ** occurs in dark parking garages and alley ways, giving the city a somber quality. Other scenes occur on or underneath the Alaskan Way viaduct which adds to the film's murky and shady tones. Unlike other films that have been shot in

Seattle, director John Sturges uses the city for more than just an attractive backdrop. Chase scenes (and there are plenty), venture beyond the cozy confines of downtown to Beacon Hill, Pill Hill and Capitol Hill with Dearborn Street, James Street and Interstate 5 as the main conduits.

McQ provides a glimpse of a real "blue collar" Seattle. Cops eat at diners advertising "Good Food" and drink their coffee black; no foam, no decaf. McQ himself lives on a boat at a Fremont Dock just below the Aurora Bridge; a far cry from the trendy Westlake houseboat that would serve as "mi casa" for Tom Hanks 20 years later in **Sleepless in Seattle**. When Lois stops by McQ's boat shortly after her husband's funeral, he pours them both a stiff bourbon and water. There are no microbrews in the Duke's fridge.

The film is also blessed with some classic images of mid-seventies Seattle. A Sonics - Lakers basketball game forms the backdrop for a meeting between McQ and Rosey the informant (played by Roger E. Mosley, before his television fame as one of Tom Selleck's sidekicks in **Magnum P.I.**) These were the days when the Sonics wore their all-gold home uniforms, when Fred Brown's afro was almost as high as the arc on his jump shot, and when Bill Russell really did seem like the ticket to an NBA championship.

Former local television news anchor Jim Harriott makes a cameo, a painful reminder of the glory days of local television when Don McGaffin was the hardest edged investigative reporter in town, and Charley Royer commented on policy rather than made it. In another cameo David Huddleston plays the role of "Pinky," a local private investigator with whom McQ goes into business after he quits the police force. Huddleston's son Michael later appears as a cab driver in the film **Bombs Away**, making them the only father and son acting team to appear in films shot on location in Seattle. Too bad junior didn't inherit any of his father's acting talent.

What Others Said

"McQ is like a dull fifties movie. Directed at a funereal pace by John Sturges..., the picture is a distended version of the other right-wing police thrillers (which were popular at the time)."

Pauline Kael

"Mr. Wayne should stick to Westerns; he's simply too slow to play any kind of policeman. Horseless in the streets of Seattle, he looks as though he needs a shot of sand."

Nora Sayre, New York Times

Summary

Although **McQ** is only a standard cop thriller and not one of Wayne's best films, the movie is worth a closer look for Seattle film fans. The attraction comes not from the Duke's thespian prowess, but from viewing aspects of the city that have mostly disappeared. In our evolution to the "big time," we seem to have lost sight of many of the simple customs and pleasures that once made downtown Seattle a true social and cultural crossroads. **McQ** is a reminder of the price we sometimes pay for progress.

"Double tall skinny, no foam." **Movie Market Photos.**

SCORCHY
(American International-1976)

Cast:	CONNIE STEVENS (Jackie Parker), CESARE DANOVA (Philip Bianco). WILLIAM SMITH (Carl Heinrich), NORMAN BURTON (Chief Frank O'Brien), GREG EVIGAN (Alan), NICK DIMITRI (Steve)
Director:	Hikmet Avedis
Producer:	Hikmet Avedis
Screenplay:	Hikmet Avedis
Music:	Igo Kantor
Length:	99 minutes
Released:	October 1976
Rating:	R (violence, nudity)

The Motion Picture Guide calls **Scorchy** *"Sleazy, full of bad taste, with scenes of {Connie} Stevens naked in the shower, which is where the whole film belongs." Yeah, so what's your point?* **Scorchy** *is a film that defines the "so bad that it's good" category, particularly for its use of mid-seventies "hip" clothing and the gratuitous use of classic Seattle locations. A product of the American International assembly line (which brought you the Frankie and Annette beach movies),* **Scorchy** *is indeed a cheap, poorly written, clumsy action picture, with just enough nudity to titillate high schoolers at the drive-in theater, where this film was briefly featured.*

Film Synopsis

The film opens in Rome, where a gangster named Carl Heinrich (William Smith) is disguised as a priest to consummate a drug deal. A suitably gruesome murder ensues with the phony priest and the drugs hopping the next non-stop flight to the Pacific Northwest. Here on the plane we get our first glimpse of Sgt. Jackie Parker (Connie Stevens), Seattle's own **POLICE WOMAN**. Dressed in a white pants suit with extra wide bell bottoms and platform shoes that would have made Elton John jealous, Jackie carefully watches Heinrich with the use of her trusty make-up mirror. Making his film debut, Greg (**B.J. and the Bear**) Evigan plays Alan, a flight steward on the plane who will later find his way into the messy world of international drug smuggling and Jackie Parker's bed.

Back in Seattle, grouchy police chief Frank O'Brien (Norman Burton) is chewing out a group of leisure-suited undercover cops, by telling them that "this {drug bust} is Jackie's case." One of the many mysteries of this film is why it was called "**Scorchy**." One assumes that it's a reference to Connie Stevens character, but no one ever refers to Jackie as Scorchy, nor is the word ever mentioned in any other context. We suppose that **Scorchy** was probably a catchier title than **"Aging Sex Kitten Tries to Breathe New Life Into Her Career by Taking Her Clothes Off."**

Eventually, we learn that Jackie is on the verge of busting an international heroin ring, that smuggles the "junk" into the country in antique statues which have been purchased by unsuspecting wealthy Seattleites. The leader of the ring, Philip Bianco (Cesare Danova), is a friend of Jackie's who believes she is a freelance pilot, not a police detective. Philip enlists Jackie's help in flying the heroin to a hiding place in the San Juan Islands. But wouldn't you know it, greedy turncoat Carl Heinrich tries to keep the drugs for himself. A lengthy chase through the streets of Seattle ensues as Jackie attempts to recover the drugs.

Although Jackie does get the drugs back, it's only temporary. While she and Alan are rolling around in bed, Carl breaks into her house, kills Alan and steals back the drugs. Exasperated, Bianco goes looking for Carl himself who has scheduled a rendezvous with another henchmen at the Edgewater Hotel. After another chase scene or two (they tend to mix together), Chief O'Brien and the rest of the troops corner Bianco and his drug connection at a house on Lake Washington. A climactic gun battle ensues with more carnage than a Sylvester Stallone movie.

Seattle People, Places and Things

Since the producers apparently couldn't afford a credible plot, decent acting, or production design, they substituted a liberal dose of Seattle scenery. This alone makes **Scorchy** worth a rental.

After the early Rome-to-Seattle airplane scene, the movie shifts to a panoramic view from Capitol Hill over I-5 towards downtown and the Denny Regrade. Next comes Sea-Tac, instantly recognizable to anyone who has suffered any length of time there. Carl Heinrich is met at the airport by his girlfriend Suzi, who is described as a stripper at the Doghouse Club. Of course, professional responsibility required us to visit every strip club in the Seattle area in search of the one which might have been the model, but our results are still inconclusive.

After a hard day of detective work, Jackie retreats to her Seward Park lakefront home. Clearly, director Hikmet Avedis did not realize that plot credibility would be damaged by having a Seattle police officer with a lakefront home, and in another scene, airline steward Alan with a penthouse apartment. Of course, locals know that they would really prefer to live in a squalid studio apartment in West Seattle. Nevertheless, they put Jackie in a home that even the Seattle police chief couldn't afford, and what better way to relax after a busy day (and wake up the audience), than to take a brisk skinny dip in Lake Washington in broad daylight. Scenes of Seattle are not the only gratuitous shots in this movie.

The best Seattle scenes occur in a lengthy chase scene midway through the picture. Jackie chases Carl Heinrich past the downtown Nordstrom and through Westlake. Carl lumbers up the monorail ramp with the long-since-departed Bartell's drugstore in the background. Jackie then commandeers a cab and chases the monorail through the Denny Regrade to the Seattle Center. The chase continues on foot through the Fun Forest and past a sign that advertises parking for 75 cents. Seventy-five cent parking? Oh right, this was mid-70's Seattle.

Blooper number one occurs in the next part of the big chase when Jackie and Carl have stolen cars again. Just a mere 12 seconds after leaving the Center, the cars are in the middle of downtown Seattle. They must have caught all the lights right. Down through Pioneer Square the cars careen and, somewhere in the Duwamish industrial area, Carl's car cracks up and he is forced to steal a motorcycle. The chase continues up the Alaskan Way viaduct and ends with Carl making an unsuccessful Evil Knievel-style leap toward a departing ferry boat. Splash!

A later chase scene takes place in, around, and on top of the Edgewater Hotel. Yes, the place where The Beatles stayed, where Led Zeppelin did rude things with a fish, and where the late Frank

Zappa got the inspiration for the song "Mud Shark," is immortalized once again. The chase is totally implausible with the participants leaping from rooftop to rooftop all the way to the ferry terminal. The real reason for the trip to the Edgewater appears to have been to give Suzi the stripper an opportunity to reappear and parade around topless. At this late stage, even gratuitous nudity can't bail out the film.

A short time later, the big drug exchange takes place at the Ye Olde Curiosity Shoppe, a landmark of the Seattle waterfront before trolleys and espresso. The Curiosity Shoppe has always been known for its weird displays, including a mummy. Judging from the acting in this film, the mummy could have played a lead.

What Others Said

*"**Scorchy** is a stupid, brutal, horribly acted melodrama.... It was written, directed and produced by Hikmet Avedis, which if it's a pseudonym, is the only indication of good sense connected with the movie."*

Vincent Canby, New York Times

"A turkey."

Mick Martin

Summary

By any standard of good filmmaking, **Scorchy** deserves a swift burial. Fortunately, this book does not adhere to those standards, making **Scorchy** a must-see for all **Seattle on Film** fans.

The Rest of the Sixties and Seventies

HIT
(Paramount-1973)

Another in a tiresome line of 1970's films featuring "tough cops forced to go outside the law," **Hit** stars Billy Dee Williams as a U.S. agent who seeks revenge on the Marseilles drug cartel he blames for the death of his daughter. About half-way through the film, Billy Dee finally stops in Seattle. His stay is extremely brief, pausing momentarily at the downtown ferry terminal to recruit a retired Jewish couple who run the food concession on a Washington State Ferry. Longtime character actor Sid Melton and actress Janet Brandt end-up leaving their lives as short order cooks to become the most unlikely members of Billy Dee's drug fighting army. The movie also features a wild car chase scene on the rural Eastside near Redmond as well as a few shots at the Winslow ferry terminal.

99 AND 44/100% DEAD
(20th Century Fox-1974)

This movie falls squarely into the category of "It must have seemed like a good idea at the time." A fine cast and a distinguished director conjure up a misbegotten gangster movie satire. Difficult to find in video stores and rarely shown on television, **99 and 44/ 100% Dead** richly deserves its obscurity.

The film's violence is relentless, and every gangster cliche is referenced. In one of the best minutes of the film (and unfortunately one of the first), gangsters are seen tossing a cement laden body off a pier, where it floats down to join an underwater corpse garden. After that inspired opening, the rest of the movie sinks as well.

In keeping with the gangster theme, the film shows a gritty side of Seattle, much like its far superior 1970's siblings **McQ** and

Cinderella Liberty. One of the most telling scenes has hitman Harry Crown (Richard Harris) and his apprentice Tony (David Hall), walking through Gasworks Park, before it had been reclaimed. What is striking is that there is no Space Needle in the background, thanks to the clever camera angles used by the crew. Later in the film, and for no apparent reason, members of the Seattle Police Department are seen parading down Yesler Way, providing 30 seconds of celluloid fame for half a score of Seattle's men and women in blue.

Old University District residents will appreciate the scenes filmed at University Heights Elementary School. A portion of the school is blown up, providing visceral satisfaction to many former students, and ranking it just behind Lincoln High School for the most destruction rendered to a school building for the sake of art (see our review of **Class of 1999**).

THE PARALLAX VIEW
(Paramount-1974)

A classic paranoid thriller, **The Parallax View** stars Warren Beatty as a disheveled and dissolute investigative reporter who stumbles on the grand political assassination conspiracy of all time. While often cited as a "Seattle" film, the only scenes of note are at the Space Needle, which is the site of a graphic and cleverly staged assassination, and at the Woodland Park Zoo, where the old children's train provides a rendezvous locale for Beatty and a source.

The bulk of the movie takes place in rural Washington, Los Angeles and Atlanta, as the dogged reporter peels back the layers of the conspiracy, finding himself dragged relentlessly toward a disturbing end. For fans of cult movies, **The Parallax View** is a must see, but for **Seattle on Film** buffs it is a second tier offering.

JOYRIDE
(American International Pictures-1977)

Take the children of some Hollywood stars of yesteryear, add a road trip to Alaska, season with a dash of cheesy drive-in nudity and you've got **Joyride**, a worthy successor to 1976's **Scorchy**, brought to you by the American International Pictures assembly line of "fine films." Financed by Sam Schulman (the former owner of the Seattle Supersonics), **Joyride** tells the story of four young Californians who tire of the "fast-life," and head north in search of adventure and a dream of owning their own fishing boat. After uncovering graft and corruption while working on the Alaskan oil pipeline, they are forced to quit their jobs. In retaliation, they take a pipeline employee hostage and turn to a life of crime. The remainder of the film is an extended chase scene, as the authorities pursue the intrepid band from Alaska back down to the lower forty-eight.

Although the Seattle scenes are extremely brief (Occidental Park, the Duwamish industrial area, and the Evergreen Point floating bridge), and don't appear until about two-thirds of the way through the picture, there are a few regional features worth mentioning. For example, the Alaska scenes were filmed in Rosyln, the same town which would be used more than a decade later as the location for Cicely, Alaska in the CBS-TV show **Northern Exposure**. The giant water pipe near Everett doubled as the Alaskan oil pipeline, and in one bar scene, an old Rainier "Northwest Beeragraphic" poster can be visibly seen.

The cast includes Desi Arnaz Jr. (son of Desi and Lucy), Melanie Griffith (daughter of Tippi Hedren), Robert Carradine (son of John), and Anne Lockhart (daughter of June), confirming the notion that talent does indeed skip a generation. Longtime KING-TV personality Cliff Lenz also stars as an F.B.I. agent named Henderson, who unsuccessfully pursues the foursome and ends up rolling his car. Poor Cliff. This never would have happened to John Keister.

THE TOP TEN SEATTLE FILM LANDMARKS

1. The Space Needle

The big kahuna, used whenever a filmmaker wants to announce "This is Seattle people!" Beginning as a backdrop for Elvis' World's Fair frolics, the Space Needle has been used as a backdrop for political assassination (**The Parallax View**), bungled robberies (**Bombs Away**), and countless panorama shots. Use of the needle is not automatically granted. Producers of a "film" called **Werewolf Cop** were turned down after it was learned their plans included impaling a police officer on the point of the Needle. Thank God for standards!

2 and 3. The Ferries/Elliott Bay

Two shots used to establish the fact there is a lot of water in Seattle (not to mention the bluest skies you've ever seen, but that was television and doesn't count.) Movie ferries never break down, run aground, or have back-ups. Elliott Bay is used as a romantic background or dumping ground for crashed cars and dead bodies.

4. Gasworks Park

The preeminent Seattle movie park. As a rendezvous for lovers (**Twice in a Lifetime** and **Singles**), or gun battle site (**Scorchy**), the odd angles and city views are a perfect backdrop.

5. Pike Place Market

Largely ignored in early films, the Market has become a prime spot for local color. Tom Hanks and Rob Reiner actually managed to scam a spot at the Athenian's lunch counter in **Sleepless in Seattle**, while Lori Singer managed to look totally out of place in **Trouble in Mind**.

6. The U-Dub

While the nickname is often mangled, the campus plays a central role in **The Slender Thread**, **The Changeling**, and **War Games**. Tenured professors actually appear in the classroom, a true movie fantasy.

7. The Alaskan Way Viaduct

Why a duck? Viaduct? Used to establish the gritty side of Seattle in films such as **McQ, Scorchy,** and **Trouble in Mind.** Enjoy it now before earthquake fears result in its demolition.

8. Pioneer Square

Not featured much lately, Pioneer Square is showcased in early films like **Harry in Your Pocket.** The use of Pioneer Square in **Singles** and **Disclosure** may signal a revival.

9. Ballard

Yep, the land of lutefisk is Seattle's movie neighborhood. The **Slender Thread, Twice in a Lifetime, Plain Clothes,** and **Dogfight** all featured Ballard locales, though in **Dogfight** Ballard Avenue played mid-60's San Francisco. "Rose's Cafe" from **Dogfight** (above) is now a Ballard antique store.

10. Sea-Tac Airport

Used in films too numerous to mention. Generally, Sea-Tac plays an airport (damn typecasting), but it did stand-in for an urban subway in **Seven Hours to Judgement**.

the eighties

Above: Michelle Pfieffer from the **Fabulous Baker Boys**, the film that firmly established Jeff Bridges as the King of **Seattle on Film.** **Movie Market Photos.**

Left: The Paramount Theater, buffed to perfection for its role in **Frances**. Movie company scaffolding can be seen in the lower left corner. **Peter Liddell/Seattle Times.**

THE CHANGELING
(Associated Film Distribution-1980)

Cast:	GEORGE C. SCOTT (John Russell), TRISH VAN DEVERE (Claire Norman), MELVYN DOUGLAS (Senator Joseph Carmichael), BARRY MORSE (Dr. Pemberton), CHRIS GAMPEL (Tuttle), RUTH SPRINGFORD (Minnie Huxley)
Director:	Peter Medak
Producer:	Joel B. Michaels and Garth H. Drabinsky
Screenplay:	William Gray and Diana Maddox
Music:	Rick Wilkins
Length:	113 minutes
Released:	March 1980
Rating:	PG (subject matter)

Considering Seattle's often bleak climate, one wonders why more horror movies haven't been shot here. Oh sure, there was **The Night Strangler** *television movie in the early seventies, but believe it or not,* **The Changeling** *was the first, and remains the only major motion picture to be shot on location in Seattle that falls distinctly into the horror film genre. This Canadian production was also the recipient of eight Genie Awards, the Great White North's equivalent of the Oscar.*

Film Synopsis

Veteran actor George C. Scott plays John Russell, a music professor who has recently moved to Seattle from New York to escape the memory of a tragic auto accident which claimed the lives of his wife and young daughter. As a graduate of the University of Washington, he has no trouble securing a faculty position at his alma mater. More importantly, however, Russell needs a special kind of house that will help inspire him to complete an unfinished symphony. Trish Van Devere (Scott's real-life wife) makes her second **Seattle on Film** appearance, this time as Claire Norman, an official with the Seattle Historical Society who suggests that Russell move into the old Chessman House. Although the place has been vacant for over 12 years, Russell is taken by the mansion's lovely music room and agrees to move in. As you can guess, this is a very bad choice.

It doesn't take long for Russell to realize that there is something odd about the old Chessman place. While composing at the grand piano in the music room, a key that he thought was broken plays by itself. Water runs by itself in the sinks and bathtubs, and at precisely 6:00 a.m. every morning, a deafening banging sound can be heard throughout the house. He asks Mr. Tuttle (Chris Gampel), the caretaker to investigate, but Tuttle just tells him, "It's an old house, it makes noises." Is that what Bob Vila would have said?

Despite these "warnings," Russell's curiosity pushes him farther into the dark mysteries of the mansion. After finding a hidden door behind some make-shift shelving, he discovers a long-hidden stairway to an abandoned child's room. Among the dust and cobwebs covering the nursery furniture, Russell finds a music box. When it opens, the melody that plays is the same as the melody of his unfinished symphony.

Now at this point most of us would have been long gone, but not Scott. Remember, it takes a lot more than a haunted house in Seattle to scare General Patton. He goes back to visit Claire at the historical society to get the truth about the Chessman House. She finds out about previous disturbances in the mansion and another society employee admits to him that "this house doesn't want people." Much like Seattle doesn't want too many California actors and actresses coming here to make movies and deciding to make the area a "second home."

To unravel the mystery of the house, Russell enlists the help of the local "ghostbuster" — a professor of parapsychology at the UW name Dr. Pemberton (Barry Morse). At this point, to tell you more about how Russell solves the haunted house mystery would spoil your enjoyment of the film. We'll just let you know that it involves a connection between a long ago murder in the house and a powerful U.S. Senator from Washington State.

Seattle People, Places and Things

The Changeling was filmed on location in New York City, Vancouver, B.C. and Seattle. Unfortunately, the scenes featuring the centerpiece of the film — the haunted Chessman House — were shot in Vancouver, not far from the main campus of the University of British Columbia. Consequently, the film's rating suffers modestly on our scale due to the inability of the film's producers to find a suitably scary house in the Emerald City.

Although the focus of the story is the Chessman House, the film does make use of a number of Seattle landmarks. For example, as a UW professor, Scott is filmed several times on the campus, walking on Red Square near Kane Hall, researching facts about the Chessmen House in Suzzallo Library, and teaching a music class in room 207 of the Architecture Building. Several students answered an ad in the UW Daily to appear as members of Russell's class on "advanced musical form," guaranteeing themselves a full 30 seconds of celluloid fame.

Russell and Claire can also be seen deciphering the headstones of long dead Seattlelites buried in the Lakeview cemetary near Volunteer Park. Other featured locations include Sea-Tac airport, the I-90 floating bridge, the downtown IBM Building, and the Rainier Tower, which is depicted as "Carmichael Towers," the offices of the esteemed Senator Joseph Carmichael of Washington.

Figuring prominently in the mystery of **The Changeling** is the character of Senator Carmichael, played by the late Melvyn Douglas. For locals, the parallels to Senator Warren Magnuson are obvious. Carmichael, like Maggie was a powerful politician who had served the state for over 30 years. The Senator is shown to be philanthropic towards the arts and other charities and generally beloved by the community. The parallel ends there. When John Russell's investigation starts to draw too close to him, however, Senator Carmichael is not above using his influence to punish those who would seek to bring him down. Now that would have hurt the old Municipal League rating.

Despite the serious subject matter, **The Changeling** does contain one good blooper. In an early scene, John and Claire attend a performance of the Seattle Symphony in what is purported to be a local concert hall. Although we don't pretend to be classical music experts, we are culturally-educated enough to know that the Seattle Symphony performs in the Seattle Center Opera House and that the performance scene in the film was not shot there. Of course, the credits provide the give away. The Vancouver

Symphony Orchestra was substituted for our own local musicians. Given the acknowledged prowess of our local symphony, we can only assume that director Peter Medak simply thought the Vancouver Orchestra was more spooky (or a lot cheaper).

What Others Said

"A good, scary ghost story."

Leonard Maltin

"A moderately engrossing spooky-house film, stalking its terrible secret in well-paced doses. The star is the house itself, an imposing mansion as fascinating as it is sinister."

Pittman and Swanson, Video Movies: A Core Collection for Libraries

*"**The Changeling** is never for a moment interesting. In some mysterious fashion, the filmmakers have managed to put together a movie that, as you watch it, gives you the impression you're seeing a synopsis of some other movie."*

Vincent Canby, New York Times

Summary

While **The Changeling** is no better or worse than other haunted house films like **The Amityville Horror** and **The Haunting**, the northwest locations and references do set it apart from these, and other efforts. Dark and stormy nights, the strange and foreboding Chessman House, and a clever "who done it" plot make this Seattle film an above average effort.

FRANCES
(Universal-1982)

Cast:	JESSICA LANGE (Frances Farmer), SAM SHEPARD (Harry York), KIM STANLEY (Lillian Farmer), BART BURNS (Ernest Farmer), JONATHAN BANKS (Hitchhiker), BONNIE BARTLETT (Stylist), JAMES BROADHEAD (Sargeant)
Director:	Graeme Clifford
Producer:	Jonathan Sanger
Screenplay:	Eric Bergen, Christopher DeVore, Nicholas Kazan
Music:	John Barry
Length:	141 minutes
Released:	December 1982
Rating:	R (brief nudity, language)

Seattle is no stranger to artistic tragedies, one of the most recent being the suicide of Nirvana's Kurt Cobain. During his brief career, Cobain demonstrated a fascination with Frances Farmer, a spirited and talented actress from the 1930's who came apart at the seams and was eventually lobotomized, living out her final days as a shadow of her former self. Her story made for a compelling book by Seattle Post-Intelligencer film critic William Arnold **(Shawdowlands)**, *and later, a showcase for actress Jessica Lange.*

Film Synopsis

Frances Farmer (Oscar nominee Jessica Lange), an idealistic student at West Seattle High School, first makes a national name for herself by writing an essay in 1931 about the death of God, earning the enmity of local Christians who sought to portray her as a pawn of atheistic Communists. Unbowed, she joins the University of Washington's "Division of Drama," honing her acting talents and striking up a close friendship with Harry York (Sam Shepard), a reporter for the Seattle Daily News. She confides to Harry one night that she doesn't want to be dull, average and normal — everything she dislikes about her hometown.

Eventually, Frances' acting talents lead her to Hollywood. In the Southern California film kingdom, she becomes a popular leading lady, yet her strong will brings her into conflict with the studio moguls. As noted by film critic Roger Ebert, "She was a stubborn, opinionated star who fought with the studio system, defied the bosses, drank too much, took too many pills, and got into too much trouble."

As her career begins to disintegrate, Frances' mother (played by Kim Stanley), steps in to "rescue" her daughter. In reality, her idea of rescue consists of a series of confinements in increasingly harsh mental institutions. Frances' cycle of "care" finally ends at Western State Hospital in Steilacoom, portrayed with 1940's hellish realism. She is brutalized with electro-shock treatment, and ultimately lobotomized by Dr. Walter Freeman, an entrepreneurial physician who became known as "the father of American lobotomy." What a legacy! A final note reveals that Frances lived out her final days hosting a daytime television show in Indianapolis, a hollow shell of the former "free spirit."

Fifty years after these actual events, and a decade after the film, Kurt Cobain wrote a song titled "Frances Farmer Will Have Her Revenge on Seattle." After his suicide, Seattle Post-Intelligencer film critic William Arnold noted the parallels in the lives of these two outsiders who ultimately were consumed by the very system that made them famous.

Seattle People, Places and Things

While **Frances** is definitely a "Seattle movie," the film is sparing in its use of the more obvious Seattle locations. Frances Farmer was raised in West Seattle, attending Lafayette Elementary, James Madison Junior High and West Seattle High School. Later, when Frances leaves for Hollywood, she departs by train from the King Street Station, with the Smith Tower looming in the background.

When she returns triumphantly to Seattle for the 1936 premiere of her film **Come and Get It**, the scene takes place at a beautifully restored Paramount Theater, it's marquee glowing with the majesty of an authentic 1930's movie palace. There are a number of inside shots, reminding us of what the Paramount (pre-recent remodel) looked like before it was permanently tinged by marijuana smoke from a thousand rock concerts.

In the latter part of the film, Frances reconnects with her father Ernest (Bart Burns), who is living in a flophouse which is actually the old Reynolds Hotel across from the old King County Jail. The Reynolds Hotel is now operated as a work release facility by the state Department of Corrections. There is also a shot in the picture across the front of the Roosevelt Hotel, renamed the Hollywood Roosevelt in the movie.

The most harrowing scenes in **Frances** take place inside Western State Hospital. It is hard to convey the unflinching look at the "snake-pits" that were our large mental institutions half a century ago. Arnold describes Frances' 1944 arrival: "After this brief and humiliating reception, she was tied to a toilet for several minutes and then — still nude — taken to a large bare auditorium-like room where about twenty-five sobbing and screaming patients paced about aimlessly or crouched on bare wooden benches that lined the four walls. She spent the night in this room, huddled in a corner for protection."

What Others Said

"The movie doesn't let us off the hook by giving us someone to blame. Instead, it insists on being a bleak tragedy, and it argues that sometimes it is quite possible for everything to go wrong. Since most movies are at least optimistic enough to provide a cause for human tragedy, this one is sort of daring."
Mick Martin

"Well-crafted but cold and depressing, despite impressive performances by Lange and Stanley."
Leonard Maltin

Summary

While somewhat sparse on Seattle locations (thus earning a middling rating on our scale), **Frances** is nonetheless worthwhile seeking out for its unflinching portrayal of human frailty and disintegration, and for the star-power of Jessica Lange. Just don't rent it on an evening when you need a little light comedy.

BOMBS AWAY
(Shapiro Entertainment-1985)

Cast:	PAT McCORMICK (Dispatcher), MICHAEL HUDDLESTON (Kabale), MICHAEL SANTO (P.R. Ransom), BEN TONE (Colonel), LORI LARSON (Susan), JOHN TRISTAO (J.J.), SUSAN LUDLOW (Lilian), DON HIBBARD (Uncle Ken)
Director:	Bruce Wilson
Producer:	Bruce Wilson and Bill Fay
Screenplay:	Bruce Wilson
Music:	John Tristao
Length:	91 minutes
Released:	June 1985
Rating:	Not Rated

Bombs Away! That's what the producers must have said when they released this clunker to the home video market in 1985. The film sat moldering on the shelf for years, no doubt while those responsible researched whether they could be held liable for forcing this cinematic sedative on an unsuspecting public. **Bombs Away** *was directed, co-produced and written by Bruce Wilson, who was also an assistant director to another one-man movie making machine, Hikmet Avedis, on the 1970's bomb* **Scorchy**. *What does he have against Seattle?*

Film Synopsis

The plot (and we use that term loosely), involves a 1950's-vintage atomic bomb which is mistakenly shipped to Lillian's War Surplus warehouse in Seattle. The employees of this "mom and pop" armaments store refuse to release the bomb unless the government admits its errors on national television. Military officials sent to retrieve the bomb refuse these demands and try to steal back the weapon. Madcap mayhem ensues as the bomb is chased through the streets of Seattle. As Dave Barry would say, "we're not making this up."

All of this is seen through the eyes of Kabale (Michael Huddleston), a rookie driver for the Space Needle Cab Company. Eventually,

Kabale picks up "the Colonel" (Ben Tone) and another sneaky government type named "P.R. Ransom" (Michael Santo) from Sea-Tac airport, and proceeds to get caught in the middle of the fight between the good guys (the heroic warehouse employees), the bad guys (the evil government officials) and some other guys (randomly appearing news reporters, barbershop quartets, visiting Texans, and "Uncle Ken"). Who are these people? Why are they important? We never know — or care.

The **Bombs Away** starring role is reserved for the cab company dispatcher, played by veteran comedian and long time **Tonight Show** staff writer Pat McCormick. Throughout most of the movie, McCormick is holed up in the subterranean headquarters of the Space Needle Cab Company, monitoring Kabale's progress with the help of a huge map of Seattle on which little toy cabs run back and forth. The dispatcher role seems to have been written more for the comedic talents of say a Dom Deluise, who presumably was too busy with **The Cannonball Run II** to take the role, or has more career sense than he is generally given credit for. Folks, McCormick phoned this one in.

When it looks like the government might finally get their hands back on the bomb, McCormick emerges at long last from the cab company dungeon to try and rescue Kabale, his cab, and the gang from Lillian's. Everyone chases each other up and down the Space Needle, through the Seattle Center and finally around and around the International Fountain where the bomb rolls to its final resting place and the movie abruptly and mercifully ends.

Seattle People, Places and Things

Why is this film set in Seattle? Why not? However, there are several good shots of the city and a few real bloopers. Early in the film, Enchanted Village stands-in for the Seattle Center. The switch is obvious to anyone who has visited both places. Enchanted Village has wheezing carnival rides surrounded by surrealistic painted mushrooms. The Seattle Center has wheezing carnival rides run by surrealistic painted people who have taken mushrooms.

Later, when the Lillian's employees discover the bomb, they note that it has a five-mile blast radius, meaning that they might have to go "all the way to Everett" to escape destruction. This begs the question of why the filmmakers didn't simply place the bomb in Everett in the first place (or alternatively Federal Way to the south), reckoning that the blast could be viewed as a civic improvement.

There are some good scenes of Interstate 5 approaching downtown, the Denny Regrade, lower Queen Anne Hill and a very nice shot of a pre-Columbia Tower downtown skyline from a ferry boat in Elliott Bay. Other scenes were shot in the Interbay area, at the Executive Inn and in a parking lot near King Street Station. By the time you've counted more than five landmarks, however, the pain of watching the movie has far outweighed the pleasures of recognition.

Throughout the movie there are numerous appearances by a reporter for the Seattle Times, including shots of the newspaper's front page. However, in one of the film's more schizophrenic twists, the Seattle Times reporter is later transformed into a correspondent for the fictitious KLLN-TV Channel 6. Perhaps KING, KIRO and KOMO got an advance look at the script.

What Others Said

No respectable film reviewer has bothered with this film. We can't even find it referenced in any of the major film and video review guides. However, for really die-hard **Seattle on Film** fans, we suggest that you fast forward to the end of the movie for the climactic chase through the Seattle Center. Yes, looming like Devil's Rock, the Needle comes at you from every angle. Is it a subtle psychological nod to the phallic nature of the bomb? A precursor to a gripping life-or-death struggle on the superstructure of the landmark? Or is it simply another way for this film to fill up a few more minutes just to prove that, "Yeah, we filmed this turkey in Seattle!"

Summary

Bombs Away probably wasn't exactly what the state had in mind when it set out to establish a film and video office in the 1970's.

TROUBLE IN MIND
(Alive Films-1985)

Cast:	KRIS KRISTOFFERSON (Hawk), KEITH CARRADINE (Coop), LORI SINGER (Georgia), GENEVIEVE BUJOLD (Wanda), JOE MORTON (Solo), DIVINE (Hilly Blue), DIRK BLOCKER (Rambo), GEORGE KIRBY (Lt. Gunther)
Director:	Alan Rudolph
Producer:	Carolyn Pfeiffer and David Blocker
Screenplay:	Alan Rudolph
Music:	Mark Isham (vocals by Marianne Faithful)
Length:	111 minutes
Released:	December 1985
Rating:	R (language, nudity)

Some of the films that have been shot on location in Seattle over the last two decades could just have easily been filmed in any mid-sized North American city. **Wargames, Seven Hours to Judgement, McQ,** *and* **The Hand that Rocks the Cradle** *are all good examples. However, it's hard to imagine that the fictitious "Rain City" setting of Alan Rudolph's* **Trouble in Mind** *could have been successfully filmed anywhere but Seattle. This mysterious, moody, and "disorientingly futuristic" 1985 release is considered a cult-favorite of film critics and Seattle film fans alike.*

Film Synopsis

The story begins when Hawk (Kris Kristofferson), an ex-cop, is released from prison and returns to Rain City to try and re-establish his life. He goes immediately to Wanda's Cafe, a greasy dive patronized by a variety of lost souls. Cafe proprietor Wanda (Genevieve Bujold), is an ex-lover who gives Hawk a place to stay, a table by the window, and a shoulder to cry on. Not long after Hawk's arrival, a young couple, Coop (Keith Carradine) and Georgia (Lori Singer), pull into town in a dilapidated trailer with an infant son. Coop soon meets cafe regular Solo (Joe Morton) who spends his time reciting bad poetry and fencing stolen merchandise. Coop and Solo quickly become partners in crime.

Despite his law enforcement past, the years in prison seemed to have turned Hawk into an amateur psychiatrist. He seems to delight in doling out Hallmark greeting card wisdom like "Ya gotta be nice to your friends, cause without 'em, you're a total stranger." When he begins to fall for the beautiful, but naive Georgia, Hawk waxes that "if a man looked at a woman's mouth before her eyes, he'd get fooled a lot less." Whoa, is this film deep or what?

While Hawk interchangeably tries to get his police job back and Georgia into his bed, Coop becomes more deeply involved with Solo and his gang of criminals. The further his criminal activities take him, the more bizarre his dress and hairdo become, and soon, Coop begins to look like a cross between Ziggy Stardust and Brian Setzer of The Stray Cats. In order to try and hit "the big time," Coop and Solo cross paths with Rain City's rackets boss, Hilly Blue (Divine). Hilly isn't happy that this new team is cutting into his territory and arranges Solo's murder at the same time he is agreeing to go into partnership with the two new kids on the block. Since most things in **Trouble in Mind** are not what they seem, it's only natural that Rudolph would be able to get the most famous transvestite in filmdom to appear on screen in gender-appropriate clothing.

The film's climactic scene takes place at a swank society party at Hilly Blue's mansion. Here, armed security guards mingle with Rain City low-lifes and powerful politicos while a lone violinist strolls through the crowd playing a lively tune, completely at odds with the mood of the party. Once the shooting starts, the carnage never stops, even when taken to comedic proportions. Hawk and Coop manage to get away safely and return to Wanda's Cafe, where a more mature Georgia must now choose between them, and begin the rest of her life.

Seattle People, Places and Things

Obviously, the real star of **Trouble in Mind** is Seattle as "Rain City," the role it was born to play. While locals will be able to easily spot a score of landmarks and locations like the Space Needle, the monorail and the Kingdome, each of them looks mysteriously different and "other worldly." (Well, maybe not the Kingdome which looks like, well, the Kingdome). There's a unique blend of

Asian and English languages spoken in Rain City, the monorail looks like the main urban transport system (this is fiction after all), and paramilitary troops patrol the streets with shoppers, workers and protesters. This picture is all about mood, and Seattle seems to fit the bill nicely.

Much of the film's interior action takes place at Wanda's Cafe, which was set-up in a storefront building on the south side of Blanchard, between First and Second Avenues. There are still apartments upstairs where Hawk could look down and leer at Georgia in her trailer parked in the empty lot next door. Other featured locations include the Pike Place Market Theater, the old Charlie's Tavern on Pike Street (which was also used in **House of Games**), and the container yards just south of the main ferry terminal.

The film also makes extensive use of the area surrounding the Alaskan Way viaduct, using the imposing concrete edifices to perfect Orwellian effect. The train tracks beneath King Street Station are similarly featured. Hilly Blue's mansion is actually the Seattle Asian Art Museum in Volunteer Park, which is given the full "art deco" treatment for the big society party. The sight of a 300-pound transvestite in a formal tuxedo strolling through an art museum with Kris Kristofferson on his arm, is image enough to put **Trouble in Mind** in the avant garde "Hall of Fame."

A few bloopers and oddities are worth noting. First, the Camlin Hotel is featured as the sight of a couple of depraved parties where Coop and Solo go to celebrate their criminal success. The hotel, however, is referred to as "The Cambridge" and only the first three letters of the exterior neon Camlin sign are shown. Nice try Alan! Second, while Georgia is seen fleeing some dangerous-types up the ramp from the Pike Place Market, the monorail is seen racing by overhead. We told you it was the city's main transport system.

What Others Said

"Here is a movie that takes place within our memories of the movies. The characters and the mysteries and especially the doomed romances are all generated by old films, by remembered worlds of neon signs and deserted areas down by the docks, of

sad cafes where losers linger over a cup of coffee, and lonely rooms where the lightbulb is a man's only friend."

Roger Ebert

*"**Trouble in Mind** seems to be saying something, but isn't able to break through the fog of {its} script." "The lead (actors) struggle through the mist, along with the audience, pretending they have some notion of what's going on — but nobody's that good an actor."*

Walter Goodman, New York Times

Summary

Trouble in Mind is really the first "art film" to be shot on location in the city. If you're a fan of the offbeat, quirky and unusual (and aren't all Seattlelites?), then this is a must see. For others, the film is worth viewing simply to see how the city can look in the hands of a capable cinematographer and director. Like the music of Ornette Coleman, you may find it pointless and peculiar, but **Trouble in Mind** certainly is something different.

Alan Rudolph directs Kris Kristofferson and Keith Carradine, in full "Rain City" outfits, during filming of **Trouble in Mind**. Natalie Fobes/Seattle Times.

TWICE IN A LIFETIME
(Yorkin-1985)

Cast:	GENE HACKMAN (Harry), ANN-MARGARET (Audrey), AMY MADIGAN (Sunny), ELLEN BURSTYN (Kate), ALLY SHEEDY (Helen), STEPHEN LANG (Keith), BRIAN DENNEHY (Nick), DARRELL LARSON (Jerry), CHRIS PARKER (Tim)
Director:	Bud Yorkin
Producer:	Bud Yorkin
Screenplay:	Colin Weland
Music:	Pat Metheny (title song by Paul McCartney)
Length:	111 minutes
Released:	December 1985
Rating:	R (language)

Much of the recent national attention focused on Seattle and its cultural "hipness" is based primarily on a set of tastes and values shared by the artists and professionals who live in the city. We often forget, however, that what has kept Seattle chugging along so well and for so many years, are the working class families who labor in the cities' building and manufacturing industries. While their experiences and concerns are often ignored by the dominant culture, they are brought meaningfully to life in the 1985 release, Twice in a Lifetime.

Film Synopsis

Harry MacKensie (Gene Hackman) is a middle-aged steelworker who lives in small town near Seattle. He and his wife Kate (Ellen Burstyn) have three grown children but little else in common. Their marriage is as tired and worn-out as this cliche, though it seems that neither or them are aware of it — at least not at first. The night of Harry's fiftieth birthday party, he wanders alone down to the neighborhood bar to celebrate with his drinking buddies. He had asked Kate to come along, but she'd rather stay home and watch T.V. The usual crowd at the Shamrock Tavern is there, along with a different face — Audrey (Ann-Margaret), the new barmaid.

Gradually, Harry and Audrey start seeing each other and begin to fall in love. When Kate finds out about their affair, Harry decides to move out of the family house and into an apartment with Audrey. Although Kate is hurt and angry, the bitterest resentment of his affair comes from oldest daughter Sunny (Amy Madigan). Not long after learning of her father's indiscretion, she drags her reluctant and embarrassed mother into the tavern to confront both Harry and Audrey in a "too painful to watch" public scene. "Hey Dad, in case you forgot, this is my mother," she screams. Despite her clumsy efforts to put the family back together, Harry leaves his wife and moves in with Audrey.

The remainder of the film is about the pain and adjustment that follows the break-up of a longtime marriage. Initially, Harry is exhilarated with his new life and love. After a while, though, he begins to feel a need to reconnect with his family. Audrey initially perceives this as a desire to return to Kate, but it's really more of a need to reestablish a relationship with his children, particularly Sunny. As plans intensify for his daughter Helen's (Ally Sheedy) wedding, Harry shows up at the rehearsal dinner with a gift for her, realizing for the first time that he has become an outcast in the family that only weeks ago, warmly celebrated his 50th birthday. And that's where the film ends. No happy or unhappy ending. Just the fact that some things are won or lost in the break-up of a marriage, and life goes on.

Seattle People, Places and Things

Whether conscious or not, **Twice in a Lifetime** provides a relatively accurate and charming portrait of the simple everyday customs of a working class Seattle family. The dinner table is populated with jars of ketchup, mustard, steak sauce and cans of Budweiser. It would have been too easy for director Bud Yorkin to put a can of Rainier beer on the table. But thankfully, he wasn't interested in forcing the location of the picture on his audience. Even in Seattle, it's probably more realistic to see a can of Budweiser on a working class dinner table than a bottle of Rainier. Other references to working class Seattle include the use of the small family backyard for Helen's wedding reception, and the local tavern where patrons drink schooners, not pints, and don't care whether or not their beer is "cask-conditioned."

Most of the film is set at the MacKensie house and the surrounding fictional town of Holden which is supposed to be somewhere between Tacoma and Seattle. In reality, most of these scenes were shot in and around Ballard, a fine substitute for the fictional blue collar burg. The MacKensie home is located near 51st and 3rd Avenues NW on the working class side of Phinney Ridge. The beauty parlor where Kate MacKensie works is located on Ballard Avenue just down the block from the old Al's Second Hand Furniture store. The neighborhood bar called The Shamrock Tavern is in reality, The Dubliner (at that time Chuckanut Charlie's) which is located in Fremont next to the Red Door Alehouse.

Specific Seattle scenes also abound in **Twice in a Lifetime**, primarily as a backdrop for Harry and Audrey's courtship. There's a quiet lunch at Ivar's Salmon House on the north shore of Lake Union, romantic strolls through Gasworks Park and on the Beacon Hill bluff overlooking I-5, the Kingdome and downtown. They also attend a Seahawks game in the Kingdome (the 1984 home opener by the way), shop for jewelry in Rainier Square and take a ferry ride on Elliott Bay. Perhaps nothing reinforces Harry's lifestyle transformation more than moving from his working class family home, to a funky apartment building on the east slope of Capitol Hill, with a gorgeous view back over Lake Union to Queen Anne and the Seattle Center.

The film's only blooper is centered around Harry's birthday celebration at The Shamrock Tavern, where patrons are seen imbibing in various kinds of hard liquor. While this is acceptable behavior in California bars, Washington State liquor laws would have required Harry and his buddies to stick to beer and wine. One local celebrity worth mentioning is an "audio" cameo appearance by Dave Niehaus, voice of the Seattle Mariners. As Harry and son-in-law Keith (Stephen Lang) share a relaxing moment watching T.V. after dinner, they hear the cry of "and it will fly away......" as Niehaus calls a Dave Henderson home run. The fact that the Mariners were playing well in the film should probably also be considered a blooper of sorts.

What Others Said

*"Everyday American life is so rare in the movies these days that some of the pleasures of **Twice in a Lifetime** are very simple ones. The rhythms of life and the normal patterns of speech*

seemed almost unfamiliar, after all the high-tech thrillers and teenage idiot films I've seen. This film was so sensible, perceptive, and grown-up that I almost looked for subtitles."

Roger Ebert

"A miracle of psychobanality. The movie is like a sermon on the therapeutic value of adultery, divorce, and remarriage, given by a minister who learned all he knows from watching TV."

Pauline Kael

Summary

Since most films shot in the city tend to focus on downtown and the dominant culture, it's a pleasant change of pace to watch a film like **Twice in a Lifetime**, that was filmed primarily in a Seattle neighborhood and focuses on regular people. Despite the serious subject matter, this is a film your whole family can appreciate.

Blue-collar Seattle resides in the Ballard home (51st and 3rd Ave. NW) of the MacKenzies in **Twice in a Lifetime**. (Private residence, do not disturb).

BLACK WIDOW
(20th Century Fox-1987)

Cast:	DEBRA WINGER (Alexandra), THERESA RUSSELL (Catherine), SAMI FREY (Paul), NICOL WILLIAMSON, (William Macauley), DENNIS HOPPER (Ben), DIANE LADD Etta), JOHNNY "SUGARBEAR" WILLIS (James), DAVID MAMET (Herb)
Director:	Bob Rafelson
Producer:	Harold Schneider
Screenplay:	Ronald Bass
Music:	Michael Small
Length:	103 minutes
Released:	February 1987
Rating:	R (language, brief nudity)

Black Widow is a "suspense thriller" about a female federal investigator tracking another woman who is systematically marrying and then murdering wealthy men. The suspense part of the film is over in the first ten minutes of the picture when the audience finds out the identity of the murderous "black widow." The thriller part was lost on both of us.

Film Synopsis

Alexandra or "Alex" (Debra Winger) works for the U.S. Justice Department's Special Investigation Task Force. She is a lonely workaholic who uses her computer to piece together a series of seemingly unrelated deaths of millionaires. Her theory is that the same woman has killed each of them in order to inherit their wealth. You really don't need to wait for her to figure this one out for you, because Catherine (Theresa Russell), the "black widow" of the title, has killed two husbands before Alex ever catches on to the scheme.

After the death of hubby no. 2 (a Dallas toy manufacturer played by Dennis Hopper), Catherine sets her sights on wealthy Seattle art collector William MacCauley (Nicol Williamson), supposedly one of the five richest men in the state. Here, the viewer is treated to the subtleties of how the black widow stalks her prey. She spends weeks studying northwest coast Indian art and rare coins. Then she offers to make a huge donation to a local museum with the stipulation that she be granted a position on the museum board. Of course, MacCauley is also a member of the board, and soon, Catherine is able to weave her tangled web of love, sex, marriage and death. When they first meet, he is taken by her knowledge and interest in his work but tells her that "you probably looked all of this up just to impress me." Despite this prophetic statement, MacCauley is murdered before Alex can intervene.

The final half of the film takes place in Hawaii where Catherine has flown to entangle a new suitor named Paul (Sami Frey). This time Alex is ready for her. The two women become friends and when Catherine offers to let her go out with her new boyfriend, Alex falls in love with Paul. Despite this, Paul marries Catherine and when she tries to kill him, Alex is set-up by the black widow and framed for the murder. Justice finally prevails, however, in what is supposed to be a surprise ending. Hardly.

Seattle People, Places and Things

Although **Black Widow** is somewhat unconvincing as a suspense story, the chameleon-like use of Seattle should please local film fans. Although the first half of the movie supposedly takes place in Washington D.C., New York, Houston, and Seattle, most of the film (save for some stock footage of those cities) was shot using buildings found in Seattle. For example, the old Seattle Post-Intelligencer building is used in some early scenes as the Washington, D.C. offices of the federal Special Investigation Task Force. When Alex's investigation takes her to Houston, she interviews one of Catherine's former relatives-by-marriage in a swanky hotel pool complex, for which the Four Seasons Olympic Hotel was a capable stand-in.

As for **Black Widow's** specific local color, Catherine carries out some of her background research on MacCauley at the Elliott Bay Book Company. The University of Washington's Burke Museum is also prominently featured as MacCauley's Seattle workplace. Later, Catherine and Alex find themselves together on a Washington State ferry, soaking up a breathtaking skyline view of the city. Other scenes briefly feature the UW Suzzallo Library and the Inn at the Market.

As part of her investigation, Alex poses unconvincingly as a local newspaper reporter, trying to get an interview with MacCauley. A minor blooper ensues when she introduces herself as a "reporter for the Seattle Post-Intelligencer." When was the last time anyone within a 100-mile radius of Seattle referred to the morning paper as anything other than the P-I?

A couple of cameos are worth noting. David Mamet, who would soon release his film **House of Games** in Seattle is featured as one of Alex's co-workers in a late night poker game at the office. The parallel to **House of Games** is unmistakable, since Mamet's film also features a high stakes poker game that is really part of an elaborate con. Also at the table is **Seattle on Film** legend Johnny "Sugarbear" Willis, who later appears in **House of Games**.

What Others Said

"The picture doesn't give you any shivers; it's muted, with an occasional near pornographic texture. Underneath the [film's] studied air it's merely a caper film, and the roles are so tawdry and underdeveloped that you may want to giggle at the fanciness."

Pauline Kael

"An interesting movie struggling to escape from a fatal overload of commercial considerations. When the film is over, there's the strange feeling that an opportunity was lost here."

Roger Ebert

"A handsome, stylishly crafted yarn, loaded with sexual tension, that stops just short of hitting the mark."

Leonard Maltin

Summary

For fans of film noir, **Black Widow** may be worth passing up for more substantive fare. Seattle film buffs, however, will find things to appreciate in this film as they struggle to determine which exterior locations are used to play other locales in the picture.

HARRY AND THE HENDERSONS
(Universal-1987)

Cast:	JOHN LITHGOW (George Henderson), MELINDA DILLON (Nancy Henderson), KEVIN PETER HALL (Harry), LANIE KAZAN (Irene), DAVID SUCHET (Jacques Lafleur), DON AMECHE (Dr. Wallace Wrightwood)
Director:	William Dear
Producer:	Richard Vane and William Dear
Screenplay:	William Dear, William E. Martin and Ezra D. Rappaport
Music:	Bruce Broughton
Length:	105 minutes
Released:	June 1987
Rating:	PG (cartoonish violence)

The Pacific Northwest is known worldwide for a number of things: terrific mountains; lush forests and lakes; rugged coastlines; and an abundant variety of wildlife. We're also blessed or cursed with the notoriety of being home to Sasquatch or "Bigfoot;" the legendary half-man, half-beast who roams the Cascade Mountains. Given the increasing popularity of Seattle as a location for major Hollywood films during the 1980's, it was only a matter of time before Hollywood started searching for story topics that would fit our city and its surrounding environs.

Film Synopsis

Consider **Harry and the Hendersons**, a charming family film that tells the tale of what happens when an ordinary movie family finds, adopts, falls in love with, and saves an ordinary movie sasquatch. The film begins in the Cascade Mountains where the Henderson family is heading home from a weekend camping trip. George Henderson (John Lithgow) is an avid hunter who manages the family sporting goods business. His wife Nancy (Melinda Dillon), is the perfect movie wife — understanding, wise, caring and warm, with just the right touch of spunk. Their kids are typical film brats who add little to the storyline or overall charm of the picture.

As George drives wildly down the mountain, with Nancy urging him to slow down because "Seattle's not going anywhere," he runs into the creature. Here we get our first glimpse of Harry (played by Kevin Peter Hall, who was Chewbacca in the **Star Wars** films). Created by Hollywood special effects wizard Rick Baker, Harry is a leading character who is compelling, remarkably expressive and much hairier than Robin Williams.

The Hendersons take Harry back home, where they try to domesticate the lumbering yeti. Although nosy next door neighbor Irene (Lanie Kazan), suspects that George has brought home more than pinecones from his camping trip, they manage to keep the eight foot beast hidden from view. Predictably, Harry proves to be a tad tough on the furnishings, but ultimately wins over the Hendersons and becomes a member of the family. He even manages to teach the Hendersons a thing or two about the sanctity of animal life, as he buries George's collection of stuffed hunting trophies and Nancy's mink coat in the backyard.

All's well that ends well? Not quite. Remember, this is a "Hollywood" picture and we haven't had our dose of dramatic tension. Enter Jacques Lefleur (David Suchet), a crazed French-Canadian big game hunter who is obsessed with catching the famed sasquatch. When the Henderson's license plate falls off the family station wagon after hitting Harry, Jacques uses it to trace the family to Seattle. Along the way, Jacques confides his suspicions about Harry to his old friend, Dr. Wallace Wrightwood (Don Ameche) who threw away a respectable academic career to chase Bigfoot. Old and embittered, he is now relegated to running a roadside "Bigfoot Museum" out of a dilapidated travel trailer.

Although George has now decided that Harry must be returned to his natural habitat, the creature manages to go AWOL. This leads to municipal mayhem as Bigfoot sightings are reported all over the city. George eventually finds the big guy in a downtown trash dumpster. Realizing that a happy ending is needed, George teams with Doctor Wrightwood to return Harry to his real home.

Seattle People, Places and Things

Harry and the Hendersons is one of the few films that uses Seattle culture and sights to set the mood. While the film was released only eight years ago, "Harry" already evokes a sense of nostalgia for a politically correct and "oh-so-sensitive" city. For example, the underlying morality play involves the enlightenment of George about the evils of hunting. Harry, of course, acts as his spiritual guide, feeling the pain of each of the forest creatures that George has "murdered" and hung on the walls of his home. In the end, George atones for these crimes and begs forgiveness from his eight-foot hairy confessor. Animals good, hunters bad.

Other "messages" are sprinkled liberally throughout the picture. Mrs. Henderson chides George for giving Harry sugar, and daughter Sara is a devout vegetarian. No doubt they can get Harry some turbinado on the next run to the co-op. Although they let Harry watch television (which is not politically correct), he watches **Bedtime for Bonzo** and throws food at the screen, splattering Ronald Reagan (which is politically correct). At the conclusion of the film, Harry brings the Henderson family, Dr. Wrightwood and even the converted Jacques Lefleur together for a group hug, demonstrating that violence is no solution to our problems (even though Harry could crush a Volkswagen bug with one hand). Rumor has it that Harry later began leading drumming circles and was the opening act for Robert Bly poetry readings. While these aren't fatal flaws, the messages are delivered with all the subtlety of a flying mallet, and make parts of the film seem oddly dated.

The use of Seattle visuals is paltry in early scenes, but picks up substantially in the second half of the film. After a gratuitous skyline shot to establish the Seattle location, much of the early action takes place at the Henderson's house at "437 Manning Drive." Camera angles make it difficult to identify the location, but later shots place the house in Wallingford. Other scenes take place in Hawthorne Hills near Laurelhurst, downtown near Pioneer Square and under the monorail towards the Space Needle. A significant part of the final chase scene occurs on I-5 between Green Lake and the University District, and on the Evergreen Point floating bridge.

The chase scene is just one of the many bloopers that will have local Seattlelites shaking their heads. First, the Hendersons are seen driving east over the Evergreen Point floating bridge, taking Harry back to the mountains. Next, their stationwagon is seen going south on I-5 near the 45th street exit. Finally, they are seen heading north on I-5, exiting off the Lake City Way offramp which has been re-labeled "Mt. Rainier National Park."

Verbal bloopers also abound. While marking Bigfoot sightings around Seattle, Harry's father — supposedly a Seattle old-timer — tells someone to put a pin in "Queen Anne's Hill." Later while giving directions, John Lithgow tells Don Ameche to "take the I-5, we're in the Wallingford section." Didn't anyone from Seattle work on this film?

Three local cameos are worth noting. Comedian Peggy Platt plays a librarian, and Dick Foley and Dana Middleton (current and former KOMO-TV personalities), appear as newscasters. The most interesting media personality, however, is Jerry Seville; the "toast of the Olympic coast" and host of a morning television show called "**Good Morning Seattle**." Jerry definitely made us feel homesick for the old **Tony Visco Show**, "live from the Trojan Horse."

What Others Said

"William Dear, the director and co-writer, apparently decided right at the start to make [the film] into a predigested sitcom instead of exploring the Bigfoot idea more thoughtfully. The movie's basic insight is that Bigfoot is a tall Cabbage Patch doll with hair."

Roger Ebert

*"Attention must be paid when a movie is as aggressively awful as '**Harry and the Hendersons**,' though it's so pin-headed that it could be the last of its inbred line. It's not likely to spawn."*

Vincent Canby, New York Times

Summary

Aw, what do critics know? Despite some notable flaws, **Harry and the Hendersons** is an enjoyable film and a safe choice for **Seattle on Film** family viewing.

HOUSE OF GAMES
(Orion-1987)

Cast: LINDSEY CROUSE (Margaret Ford), JOE MANTEGNA
                  (Mike), MICHAEL NUSSBAUM (Joey), LILIA SKALA (Dr.
                  Littauer), J.T. WALSH (The Businessman), STEVE
                  GOLDSTEIN (Billy Hahn), RICKY JAY (George the Vegas
                  Man), MESHACH TAYLOR (Mr. Dean), JOHNNY
                  "SUGARBEAR" WILLIS (Hotel Doorman)
Director: David Mamet
Producer: Michael Hausman
Screenplay: David Mamet
Music: Alaric Jans
Length: 102 minutes
Released: October 1987
Rating: R (language, sexual situations)

A satisfying psychological drama, **House of Games** *also
provides subtle treats for the fan of Seattle film locales. As
local film critic Robert Horton writes, "Welcome to
Underground Seattle. Not the guided tour through the
basements of Pioneer Square, but a much more elusive location."
Seedy downtown storefronts and a locally famous pool hall are
used to cast "a persuasive spell, ... about the necessity of dark
places to transact dark business."   Released in 1987,* **House of
Games** *was the directorial debut of renowned playwright
David Mamet.*

Film Synopsis

As the film opens, we meet Dr. Margaret Ford, played by Mamet's
then love interest Lindsey Crouse.   Dr. Ford is an obsessive,
compulsive psychiatrist who has written a book on — surprise —
obsessive, compulsive behavior. One of her patients, an obsessive,
compulsive gambler named Billy Hahn (Steve Goldstein) tells her
he fears he will be murdered over a large gambling debt. Margaret
talks him out of suicide and offers to help him square accounts with
his bookie. Ford's offer leads her to Mike, the leader of a ring of
confidence men, played with obsessive, compulsive intensity by
Joe Mantegna. He appears intrigued by her boldness and interest
in his work, and offers her a deal: she must help him fool a visiting

Vegas gambler in a high stakes poker game and he will forgive Billy's gambling debt. Agreeing to his terms, Margaret becomes fascinated with Mike's criminal professionalism, and is drawn deeper into the dangerous but seductive world of the con. **House of Games** has twist after twist after twist, and we won't spoil the film by giving away any more details about the plot.

While the storyline is satisfyingly complex, it's the performances and Mamet's dialogue that really make **House of Games** crackle. Mamet is a master at capturing the blunt, coarse language of the darker side of life. Now at this point, we have to be perfectly honest. We watched this one on the KOMO "**Fourmost Movie**" so we're guessing that there was blunt, coarse language. In most Mamet plays or films, every other word begins with the letter "F." This film appears to be no exception, because at certain points, there was so much looping of acceptable substitutes that it began to look like a poorly dubbed Kung Fu movie.

Still, we have nothing but praise for the "**Fourmost Movie**;" for decades, a purveyor of adequate films in the lonely hours of the morning. Also, whether conscious or not, the "**Fourmost Movie**" seems to specialize in films with a Seattle connection — either the movie was filmed here, or something in the picture evokes nostalgia for the city.

Seattle People, Places and Things

House of Games doesn't advertise its Seattle location. There are no lingering skyline shots, no obligatory Space Needle backgrounds, no gratuitous local media references. Instead, there is rain, and a dark, moody atmosphere. **House of Games** conjures up strong percolator coffee, despairing jazz, and two days' stubble. Everyone chain-smokes and no one worries about it. There is nary a sprout, Birkenstock or Yanni CD in sight. As film critic Roger Ebert said, "the characters and others [in **House of Games**] live in a city that looks, as the Seattle of **Trouble in Mind** did, like a place on a parallel time track. It is a modern American city, but like none we have quite seen before; it seems to have been modeled on the paintings of Edward Hopper, where lonely people wait in empty public places for their destinies to intercept them." This atmosphere is enhanced by the use of tight character shots, dark lighting, and gloomy wet weather.

Because the film does not trumpet its location, it is difficult to ferret out distinctive locations. The patient viewer (who has a quick finger on the rewind button), will be rewarded. Much of the movie takes place at or near the **House of Games**, an enormous, seedy upstairs tavern and pool hall that was the old downtown 211 Club. The address in the film is 211 Beaumont but the real location was at Second and Union. The club was torn down for the Metro bus tunnel shortly after **House of Games** was filmed. During the day, the 211 Club was a popular lunch spot with government workers in the nearby Arcade Plaza Building and other locations. During the evening, it took on an entirely different feel — acres of green felt enveloped in incandescent light and cigarette smoke. The 211 Club has since moved further up Second Avenue to a new Belltown location; thankfully, the tables, smoke and atmosphere remain largely the same.

In another scene, Mike's gang of con artists show Margaret some simple tricks while standing on the sidewalk in front of the old Embassy porno theater, just across the street from the original 211 Club. A large G.O. Guy drugstore sign still hangs on the corner, a reminder of the rapidly vanishing Seattle middle-class retail community. Mike's gang of con men hang out at the old Charlie's Tavern near the downtown Sheraton Hotel. Later, Margaret and Mike stroll down the sleazy side of First Avenue, passing the Zorba the Buddha porno "church," and the American Liberty adult bookstore. This is First Avenue the way it was meant to be — Raincoat Men instead of Hammering Man.

Throughout the movie, the tightly wound and repressed Dr. Ford falls further under the spell of the charismatic Mike, whose crystalline amorality shakes her professional correctness. After enough erotic tension has been built, Margaret and Mike end up at the Four Seasons Olympic Hotel, procuring the keys to room 1138. Because we watched this one on the **"Fourmost Movie,"** we really don't know if the love scene was worth watching, but it soon gives way to more plot twists. Other clearly recognizable Seattle locations include the parking lot at the Kennedy Hotel on Fifth Avenue, and an abnormally deserted Sea-Tac airport, which hosts the climactic scene.

Three small roles are worth noting. Ricky Jay appears early in the film as a Vegas card shark. Jay, who also consulted on the movie, is a master magician and practitioner of the con, and his books on the subject are worth reading. Also, a "pre-**Designing Women**" Meshach Taylor appears in a small role as a member of Mike's gang. The crowd he hangs out with here is a long way from Sugarbaker's, even if some of the characters are as annoying as Delta Burke. Finally, Johnny "Sugarbear" Willis capitalized on his crisp repartee with David Mamet in **Black Widow**, and was cast as a hotel doorman here.

What Others Said

"This movie is awake. I have seen so many films that sleepwalk through the debris of old plots and secondhand ideas that it was a constant pleasure to watch **House of Games.***"*

Roger Ebert

"Mr. Mamet, poker player and Pulitzer Prize-winning playwright, makes a fine, completely self-assured debut."

Vincent Canby, New York Times

Summary

Overall, **House of Games** has plenty to satisfy the most discriminating **Seattle on Film** buff. It is a movie that rewards close attention to detail. Seemingly inconsequential bits of business later turn out to be pivotal, and the moody atmosphere reinforces the film's bleakly fascinating outlook. If you can't find it on the "**Fourmost Movie**," this one is definitely worth a full-price rental. (You'll even hear the "F" words).

PLAIN CLOTHES
(Paramount-1988)

Cast:	ARLISS HOWARD (Nick Dunbar), SUZY AMIS (Robin Torrance), GEORGE WENDT (Chet Butler), DIANE LADD (Jane Melway), SEYMOUR CASSEL (Ed Malmburg), JACKIE GAYLE (Coach Zeffer), ABE VIGODA (Mr. Wiseman), ROBERT STACK (Principal Gardner), ALEXANDRA POWERS (Daun-Marie Zeffer), HARRY SHEARER (Simon Feck), LOREN DEAN (Matt Dunbar)
Director:	Martha Coolidge
Producer:	Richard Wechsler and Michael Manheim
Screenplay:	A. Scott Frank
Music:	Scott Wilk
Length:	98 minutes
Released:	April 1988
Rating:	PG (language)

Before it comes apart at the end, **Plain Clothes** *is an enjoyable, if implausible, comedy/murder mystery. Coming at the end of the "brat pack wave," the film was the victim of bad timing, and received a less than enthusiastic response by moviegoers. Pass straight thru theaters, go directly to video, and do not collect millions in ticket sales.*

Film Synopsis

Nick Dunbar (Arliss Howard) is a baby-faced undercover Seattle police officer who has been relegated to impersonating ice cream truck drivers in order to catch street thugs. That all changes when Dunbar's younger brother Matt (Loren Dean) is accused of murdering a hated teacher at his high school. After an altercation with the homicide cop assigned to his brother's case, Nick gets suspended from the force. To try and clear his brother of the murder charge, Nick goes deep undercover, disguised as a high school student.

Posing as "Nick Springsteen," a transfer student from Delaware who claims to be a "distant cousin," Nick enrolls at Adlai Stevenson High School. With help from his brother, and his partner Ed (Seymour Cassel), who pretends to be his father, Nick slowly begins to gain the acceptance of his high school classmates, not to mention his beautiful young English teacher Robin Torrance (Suzy Amis). Other high school "characters" encountered by Nick include Robert Stack as the school principal who "plays by his own rules," Abe Vigoda as Mr. Wiseman, the senile math teacher, and Diane Ladd as the "see-all, know-all" school secretary, Jane Melway.

In an attempt to "heighten" the mystery, director Martha Coolidge throws out enough red herrings to fill a Ballard fishing trawler. Soon, three main plot lines begin to emerge leading to three different suspects. First, a group of teachers is involved in a scam to defraud the teacher's pension fund. Second, a bizarre shop teacher named Chet Butler (played by George Wendt), pops up making veiled references to a guilty past and showing his students "a million and one uses for bowling pins." Third, satirist Harry Shearer appears several times as attorney Simon Feck, a twitchy and wordless man who arouses suspicion just by his presence. While most of these threads are tied together by the end of the film, the solution to the mystery feels more like a contrivance to finish the movie, rather than a carefully plotted twist.

The messy mystery is forgivable, however, because the film is brutally realistic in its depiction of high school as a particularly awkward and hellish time of life. Most people who are honest with themselves, would never want to go back to high school, and **Plain Clothes** provides ample reasons why. Teachers are depicted as generally dim and corrupt, and school administrators are pettifogging bureaucrats. Students are alternately nerdish or cruel — indeed Nick's greatest tormentors are a student security force of young fascists known as "The Wardens."

Seattle People, Places and Things

While Seattle is not trumpeted as the location for **Plain Clothes**, there are plenty of local references and locations to satisfy Seattle film fans. Most of the movie takes place at the Monroe Center in Ballard, the fictitious Adlai Stevenson High School in the film. Near the end of the picture, the Center's back parking lot is converted into a large carnival for the school "Mayfest." Over the entry to the Mayfest flies a large banner saying "Welcome Pagans." Any true Seattlelite knows this would never happen at a real Seattle school because (1) it would cost money, (2) it would be raining, and (3) Seattle School District policy would require that more than pagans be welcomed to avoid excluding any other group.

At one point, Nick meets his partner Ed (prominently wearing his Seahawks jacket), at the Athens Restaurant, a great old neighborhood gathering spot on Queen Anne Hill. There are a number of shots of residential homes in Wallingford, the Ballard industrial area, the King County Courthouse and Salmon Bay Park in the Ballard/ Crown Hill area. One small touch, which will be dear to readers of Byron Fish's old column in the Seattle P-I, has Fish's "Free at Last" poster in Principal Gardner's office. The picture shows a little old man throwing his clothes off and running naked into the sunset, and has been a favorite of soon-to-be retirees for years. Another nice touch places the location of a teacher's pension fund meeting at 220 Little Mt. St. Helen's Road. Too bad the movie wasn't as explosive.

One blooper worth mentioning involves shop teacher Chet Butler's complaint to Nick that he was a school counselor before his funding was cut by "Proposition 9." Now folks, let's review a little Washington State civics. California has Propositions and we have Initiatives. Sure, we cut funding for public schools just the same, but let's get those references correct.

What Others Said

"Unless they're uncommonly good, back-to-high school movies have a way of making audiences count the minutes till graduation, and certainly that's the case with Plain Clothes."

Janet Maslin, New York Times

"A marvelously tongue-in-cheek hybrid of mystery, teen comedy, and suspense thriller."

Mick Martin

Summary

In sum, **Plain Clothes** gets a passing grade, less for its mystery than for its evocation of high school hell.

SEVEN HOURS TO JUDGEMENT
(Trans World Entertainment-1988)

Cast:	BEAU BRIDGES (John Eden), RON LEIBMAN (David Reardon), JULIANNE PHILLIPS (Lisa Eden), AL FREEMAN, JR. (Danny Larwin), TINY RON (Ira), REGGIE JOHNSON (Chino), GLEN-MICHAEL JONES (Doctor), CHRIS GARCIA (Victor), JOHNNY "SUGARBEAR" WILLIS (Officer Wilton), JANE BRAY (T.V. Reporter)
Director:	Beau Bridges
Producer:	Mort Abrahams
Screenplay:	Walter Davis
Music:	John Debney
Length:	96 minutes
Released:	September 1988
Rating:	R (violence, language)

By the late 1980's, about two major motion pictures per year were being shot on location in Seattle. Compared to the previous decade when the average was less than one, it's obvious that movie producers were beginning to think of Seattle less as a unique, picturesque location shoot, and more of a capable backlot for complete productions. How else to explain Seven Hours to Judgement; *a film about abduction and injustice that goes out of its way to deny that it was shot in Seattle.*

Film Synopsis

Beau Bridges both stars and directs (he should have chosen one or the other), in this story of John Eden (Bridges), a prominent big city judge whose wife is kidnapped by a distraught husband whose own wife was brutally murdered by four members of a street gang called the "Icemen." In the film's early scenes, we discover that Judge Eden also has a promising political future. His friend and political advisor Danny Larwin (Al Freeman, Jr.) encourages him to make a run for the U.S. Senate. Lisa Eden (Julianne Phillips), his beautiful wife, is totally devoted to him, his career, and keeping herself in great shape. Everything in John Eden's life seems perfect and headed for bigger and better things.

Yet, hanging over his head is the upcoming trial of the thugs accused of attacking and murdering Ellen Reardon, the wife of David Reardon (Ron Leibman) who owns several local audio-video stores. Reardon, who also serves as his company's pitchman in the guise of "Ravin' Reardon - King of Low Prices" (Jack Roberts perhaps?), pays a visit to Judge Eden's chambers to beg for more time to prepare the prosecution's case against the gang members. When Eden refuses and the charges against the Icemen are dropped due to a lack of evidence, "Ravin' Reardon" proves to be even more crazy than his commercial persona.

Shortly after the trial ends, Reardon abducts Lisa while she is shopping downtown. Then, masquerading as a waiter, he kidnaps the judge from a political fundraiser and takes him to an abandoned warehouse where by video link-up, Eden can see his wife drugged and confined in an old rundown hotel. Once there, Reardon makes the judge a proposition. If Eden will retrieve a critical piece of evidence that can prove the gang members murdered his wife, he will let Lisa live. The only catch is that it must all be done within seven hours. Get it? Seven hours to judgement; ....dum, dum, dum, daaaahhhh!

The remainder of the film consists mostly of watching Beau Bridges race through the streets of Seattle looking for the various characters who hold the clue to the missing piece of evidence. First, it's over to some part of the city called "Spanish Town," to check in with a Hispanic gang who have an axe to grind with the Icemen. Then it's down underneath the city for a ride on the subway. The fact that Seattle has a subway should come as a great relief to regional transit planners.

After obtaining the key evidence, Eden returns to the warehouse where Ravin' Reardon has rigged an elaborate series of "booby-traps" to prevent him from meeting the seven-hour deadline. Eden manages to elude most of Reardon's "house of horrors" and after a climactic gun battle, John and Lisa emerge safely from the warehouse into the dawn of a new day. Orchestra please.

Seattle People, Places and Things

Although Seattlelites will have no trouble spotting a variety of local landmarks, **Seven Hours to Judgement** is definitely a film in a state of complete "Emerald City" denial. Panoramic shots of downtown intentionally mask any view of the Kingdome, ferry boats, or heaven forbid, the Space Needle. Street signs have been altered so that the downtown grid pattern matches alternating letters and numbers. Third and Pike becomes Third and C, and so on. Television weathermen forecast another several days of recordbreaking high temperatures, and the local newspapers are referred to as The Daily Register and The Daily Tribune. Where is this place?

The most obvious attempt at differentiating the city in the film from Seattle is the existence of a subway. Now where do you suppose producer Mort Abrahams found a subway in Seattle? If you guessed Sea-Tac, you win a year's worth of canned salmon. The airport's underground terminal shuttle trains were transformed into a big city subway where much of the film's action takes place. The effect, however, is somewhat unconvincing. Most of us are conditioned to seeing big city subways as dark, dirty and foreboding places. Despite some fake turnstiles and transit posters, the Sea-Tac trams just look too squeaky clean and well-lit to pass as an underground urban thoroughfare. Instead, you just keep wondering why the subway passengers aren't more concerned about catching their flights on time.

Despite the well-intentioned efforts of the producers to keep the "Seattleness" out of the picture, some local landmarks do manage to peep-thru. In one scene the Pike Place Market sign is clearly visible in the background. The downtown federal courthouse on Fifth Street doubles as, guess what? — the courthouse, where Judge Eden hears the Reardon murder trial. Eden's political reception takes place in the lobby of the Sorrento Hotel. Other scenes were filmed in the residential neighborhood near Volunteer Park (Judge Eden's home is the big white mansion on Prospect Avenue), Beacon Hill and downtown near Rainier Square and the 5th Avenue Theater.

During John Eden's nocturnal seven hours of judgement, he visits a dive called the "El Pollo" near the old House of Fabrics and Glen Hotel on Third Avenue between Union and Pike. This serves as the headquarters of the Grandes gang in "Spanish Town." The warehouse where Reardon initially takes Judge Eden and subsequently uses as his "little shop of horrors" is located on

Occidental Avenue, just across the walkway from the NW corner of the Kingdome. In one of the films few real bloopers, Eden escapes the police in the "Sea-Tac" subway by dashing down into the utility tunnels. From there, he literally falls into Underground Seattle below Pioneer Square — a mere 20 miles to the north.

Two small roles are worth noting. First, the king of Lesser Seattle Cinema, Johnny "Sugarbear" Willis, appears as Officer Wilton, the policeman who witnessed the murder of Ellen Reardon. Second, Jane Bray appears sporadically as a T.V. news reporter. You might remember Jane from her powerful performance as an army lieutenant in **Bombs Away**. Then again, you might not.

What Others Said

"Bridges directs himself in an earnest but farfetched revenge saga as the hapless judge whom nut case Leibman feels had been too lenient with the minority punks who killed Leibman's wife."

Leonard Maltin

"A dim suspense drama. The screenplay holds less water than a ravaged buttercup."
Vincent Canby, New York Times

"An action-thriller that loses much of its thrill due to its baby-faced star (and his jumpy direction)."
Mick Martin

Summary

As Seattle grows more popular as a destination for Hollywood filmmakers, we can expect more films like **Seven Hours to Judgement**. And isn't that the way longtime Seattlelites would like it? No sense advertising local attractions and turning each film into a real estate marketing video for out-of-town speculators. So let's hear the cry Seattle, "No More Space Needles on film!"

SAY ANYTHING
(20th Century Fox-1989)

Cast:	JOHN CUSACK (Lloyd Dobler), IONE SKYE (Diane Court), JOHN MAHONEY (James Court), LOIS CHILES (Mrs. Court), JOAN CUSACK (Constance), LILI TAYLOR (Corey Flood), AMY BROOKS (D.C.), PAMELA SEGALL (Rebecca)
Director:	Cameron Crowe
Producer:	Polly Platt
Screenplay:	Cameron Crowe
Music:	Richard Gibbs, Anne Dudley and Nancy Wilson
Length:	100 minutes
Released:	April 1989
Rating:	PG-13 (language, sexual situations)

A brilliant directorial debut from rock journalist Cameron Crowe, **Say Anything** *captures the false starts and eventual triumph of a most unlikely love affair. Taken with his other Seattle film,* **Singles,** *Crowe proves an adept observer of the joys and sorrows of young relationships in his adopted home.*

Film Synopsis

Lloyd Dobler (John Cusack) is a well-liked, but somewhat ordinary teenager. He has just graduated from high school, and is determined to date Diane Court (Ione Skye), the beautiful and brilliant class valedictorian. Showing more self confidence than anyone his age has a right to, Lloyd calls Diane and talks her into a date.

While Lloyd's friends are skeptical — they refer to Diane as "a brain trapped in the body of a game show hostess" — they marvel as Diane falls for Lloyd's honest and playful approach. Her protective father (John Mahoney) does not approve, partly because Lloyd is not the rich preppie he envisioned for his daughter, partly because he fears Diane's new love will interfere with a prestigious scholarship she has won, and mostly because Lloyd's career ambition is to be a kickboxer.

It turns out that Dad has a lot more to worry about than Lloyd. For years he has been skimming from the old folks living in the nursing home that he runs, and the IRS is about to catch up with him. The bulk of the film focuses on Diane's struggle to cope with her love for Lloyd as her father's life crumbles around her. Early in the film, it becomes clear that Diane and her Dad have an unusually honest relationship — they note that they can "say anything" to each other. Part of the film's twist is that quirky Lloyd turns out to be truly honest in his love for Diane, while dear old Dad deceives everyone in the name of fatherly love.

Lloyd and Diane's relationship is full of the awkward stops and starts of young love. Some of the films richest moments come when they experience each other's world — Diane attends her first kegger (remember keggers?) and Lloyd visits Diane during her shifts at the nursing home. They learn much about themselves through each other, and the seeming mismatch turns out to be a perfect match indeed.

Seattle People, Places and Things

While Cameron Crowe made more extensive use of Seattle in his next film **Singles, Say Anything** has just enough local color to reward the patient **Seattle on Film** viewer. The picture opens with a montage of Seattle scenes, including Ballard, the Aurora Bridge south towards Queen Anne, the Auditorium Cleaners in Fremont (which also appears in **The Hand that Rocks the Cradle**), and the Waiting for the Interurban sculpture near the Fremont Bridge.

The most impressive shots of Seattle come during the night of the kegger, as Lloyd and Diane tour the city trying to get an inebriated guest back home. Soon after they leave the party, there's a great shot of downtown Seattle looking north from the south end of the Alaskan Way viaduct. By the time their guest finally sobers up and remembers where he lives, it's dawn and the city is covered in an ethereal early morning mist — or maybe it was an ethereal fog. Depends on your perspective. Mist is enchanting and romantic (ala **Brigadoon**), and fog is, well, fog. Yeah, this is Seattle. It was fog.

By the time he filmed **Singles**, Crowe had managed to avoid any careless location bloopers. Fortunately for us, there are a couple worth noting in **Say Anything**. During an extended cruise in his car contemplating his relationship with Diane, Lloyd passes by the

Guild 45th Theater in Wallingford, and then immediately passes by the Bellevue Square shopping mall. That's better time than we ever made on the Evergreen Point floating bridge — ain't moviemaking grand. In another location blooper, Lloyd cruises by Tacoma's famed landmark, the Java Jive. We doubt that Tacoma would let Seattle steal its only remaining cultural treasure, now that Ivan has been shipped off to Atlanta.

The film also has a bit of post hoc cross-pollination. John Mahoney now plays Frasier's father in the NBC sitcom set in Seattle, and Bebe Neuwirth, who played Frasier's wife Lillith on **Cheers**, also has a small role here.

What Others Said

*"**Say Anything** is one of those rare movies that has something to teach us about life. It doesn't have a "lesson" or "message," but it observes its moral choices so carefully that it helps us see our own. That such intelligence could be contained in a movie that is simultaneously so funny and so entertaining is some kind of miracle."*

Roger Ebert

*"The predictable surface of **Say Anything**, is constantly being cracked by characters who think and talk like real people and by John Cusack's terrifically natural, appealing Lloyd."*

Caryn James, New York Times

"A lovely piece of work," pointing out that you won't *"feel like a ninny for watching a high-school movie."*

Pauline Kael

Summary

Seattle's second high school film in as many years, **Say Anything** is far superior to its **Plain Clothes** predecessor. Honest, likeable and just a wee bit weird, Lloyd Dobler offers a portrait of what we'd like to think is the prototypical Seattle nice guy. And in this film, nice Seattle guys do finish first.

THE FABULOUS BAKER BOYS
(20th Century Fox-1989)

Cast:	JEFF BRIDGES (Jack Baker), BEAU BRIDGES (Frank Baker), MICHELLE PFEIFFER (Susie Diamond), ELLIE RAUB (Nina), XANDER BERKELEY (Lloyd), DAKIN MATTHEWS (Charlie), KEN LERNER (Ray), ALBERT HALL (Henry)
Director:	Steve Kloves
Producer:	Paula Weinstein and Mark Rosenberg
Screenplay:	Steve Kloves
Music:	Dave Grusin
Length:	114 minutes
Released:	October 1989
Rating:	R (language, adult themes)

A sentimental ode to the glory days of lounge entertainment, **The Fabulous Baker Boys** *is both an audio and visual treat. Anyone old enough to remember (and appreciate) Seattle entertainers Phil Stumpo, Primo Kim, Walt Wagner, and the venerable Patti Summers, will be instantly drawn to the ambiance and nostalgia of this picture. The film represented the directorial debut of writer Steve Kloves. Coincidentally, the film's executive producer, Sydney Pollack, also made his directorial debut in a Seattle picture; 1965's* **The Slender Thread.**

Film Synopsis

Frank and Jack Baker (Beau Bridges and Jeff Bridges) have been playing together as the "Baker Boys" twin-piano nightclub act for 15 years. Frank, the older and less musically talented brother, manages the business and handles the onstage banter. He's the stable one whose married with kids, and sees music as nothing more than a steady paycheck. Jack, the real musician in the family, is so depressed and bored with his life and the act that he can barely play "The Girl from Ipanema" without snarling. Single, he lives in a rundown flat with only an old dog and the little girl from the upstairs apartment to keep him company. His real pleasure comes from stealing away on his nights off to play in a local jazz club.

To Frank and Jack, now in their forties, "The Baker Boys" act has become as routine and familiar as brushing their teeth, and almost as much fun. The nightclub gigs come in sporadically, and one manager even pays them not to appear on the second night. Desperate to turn their fortunes around, Frank suggests taking on a female vocalist. After auditioning 37 different singers (none of whom can carry a tune), in walks Susie Diamond (Michelle Pfeiffer). While she's foul-mouthed, crude and street savvy, Susie can sing like a songbird. As she croons "Ten Cents a Dance," Frank and Jack can sense the magic that she could bring to the act.

With Susie on board, the Baker Boys' popularity is rejuvenated. They're booked into the classiest clubs in town, and the lounges are crowded with appreciative audiences. Although Susie is still a little rough around the edges, Jack still depressed with his life, and Frank treating them both like children on a school campout, these differences are ignored in the glow of their new found success.

For the New Year's holiday, the gang plays at a swanky resort outside of town. After a couple of nights, Frank is called home on a family emergency, leaving Jack and Susie to finish the gig by themselves. Without the boss around, the two get a chance to shine as a duo. They drop the cheesier songs from the act (no Feelings), and light up the room with new material and energy. Slowly, they begin to fall in love.

When Frank finds out, he reasserts control and demands that they do things the old way. Susie, who knows about Jack's secret love for jazz and distaste for the nightclub scene, looks to him to back-up her desire to change the act. Lacking the energy to cross his big brother, Jack acquiesces to Franks' demands. Angry and hurt, Susie decides to leave the act. When the boys try to continue on, the gigs are even worse than before. After playing a telethon at three o'clock in the morning on Channel 71, Jack unloads on Frank and a decade and a-half of anger and resentment explode in the parking lot outside.

Realizing now that the Baker Boys act is finished, Frank and Jack decide to go their separate ways. Frank will teach piano in the suburbs while Jack will try and make it as a jazz musician. In the film's final scene, Jack reconnects with Susie to apologize and try to start over. "Do you think you'll see me again?" she asks him.

"Yeah, I do think I'll see you again," calls Jack, as Susie saunters elusively down the street.

Seattle People, Places and Things

The Fabulous Baker Boys is a cinematic celebration of Seattle's nightlife, harkening back to the days when the old town was often referred to as the "City of Lights." Neon reflections on wet pavement, timeless ballads, and rumpled tuxedos in smoky lounges help to set the film's prevailing mood. Although the current definition of "Seattle nightlife" generally means catching some alternative band at the Crocodile Cafe or the Offramp, there was a time when going out for a night on the town meant Phil Stumpo at The Wharf or Primo Kim at the Edgewater. If you were in the mood for comedy, it might have been northwest favorite Pete Barbutti or Harry Taylor (remember him?) — "the funniest man in Seattle." Although many of the nightclub scenes were filmed in Hollywood (including the now famous "Makin Whoopee" scene, with Michelle Pfeiffer slinking atop the piano), there are enough shots in and around the Four Seasons, Roosevelt Hotel, and the old Trader Vic's to authenticate the northwest lounge environment.

Like its predecessor **House of Games**, much of **The Fabulous Baker Boys** focuses on lesser known parts of the city, avoiding (for the most part), more famous and photogenic local landmarks. For example, the opening sequence in the picture follows Jeff Bridges as he strolls from Belltown via First Avenue, past the Lusty Lady adult theater, and on to a gig at an unspecified downtown nightclub. Other scenes take place in and around Pioneer Square, uptown between Eighth and Ninth north of Pike, and the west slope of Capitol Hill near Westlake. Despite the "lesser Seattle" focus, director Kloves just couldn't help sneaking in a shot of the monorail and ferry boats on Elliott Bay at night.

A lot of the interior action occurs in Jack's rundown apartment. In actuality, his flat is the top floor of Masin's Furniture on the corner of Second and Main. The film contains several wonderful daytime and evening shots from the top of the building featuring Beacon Hill, King Street Station, the Smith Tower and the Duwamish industrial area. The picture's only blooper comes right at the beginning of the film. During Jack Baker's jaunt from his girlfriend's apartment to a gig with brother Frank, he manages to exit Ivar's Acres of Clams just after he is seen strolling through the main concourse of the Public Market. Fast, isn't he?

What Others Said

"A romantic fantasy that has a forties-movie sultriness and an eighties movie-struck melancholy."

Pauline Kael

"A film specializing in smoky, down-at-the-heels glamour, and in the kind of smart, slangy dialogue that sounds right without necessarily having much to say."

Janet Maslin, New York Times

Summary

Nominated for four Oscars, **The Fabulous Baker Boys** is a double treat for Seattle film buffs — a great movie plus interesting locales. While the nightclub scene romanticized in the film no longer dominates, there's enough sentimentality in the film to get even the most hardcore grunge fan to stop for a quick set at the Canlis bar.

It's lush living for Jack Baker in his seedy apartment above Masin's Furniture Warehouse at Second and Main. In each Seattle film he does, Jeff Bridges moves one rung down the housing chain (see **American Heart**). Next film we expect him to live in the dumpster with Harry from **Harry and the Hendersons**.

The Rest of the Eighties

BUSTIN' LOOSE
(Universal-1981)

Richard Pryor plays a convicted thief who is ordered by his parole officer to drive social worker Cicely Tyson and a group of emotionally and physically abused kids from Philadelphia to Washington State in a school bus. Although estranged at first, Pryor eventually wins over Tyson and her brood with his own brand of "street smarts" and quick-witted humor. The film's most entertaining scene involves Pryor outwitting a band of KKK thugs by pretending that he's transporting a group of sightless children to the Ray Charles Institute for the Blind.

While **Bustin' Loose** was filmed in Washington State (primarily Redmond and Ellensburg), the only scenes of Seattle are at the beginning of the picture. Here Seattle stands in for the city of Philadelphia, and somewhat convincingly too, until a Sea-Land trailer and the Nordic Cold Storage building sign provide the giveaway. Nick Dimitri, who appeared in **Scorchy** and Vern Taylor, a local veteran of several Seattle pictures both have minor roles. The picture was shot mostly in 1979, but wasn't released to theaters until 1981 because of Pryor's near fatal accident, in which he was severely burned while free-basing cocaine.

WARGAMES
(MGM/United Artists-1983)

Wargames stars Matthew Broderick as Seattle high school student David Lightman; an exceptionally bright kid who has trouble getting along with teachers who move at about one-half his intellectual pace. His parents are typical middle-class stereotypes. Mom's a Century 21 real estate salesperson, and Mr. Lightman; well he works at that same "office" where Ward Cleaver and Ozzie Nelson went to waste eight hours a day. Dad's chief accomplishment is the invention of a clever way to butter corn on the cob.

David becomes obsessed with gaining access to what he thinks is a new line of video games from a company called Protovision. In reality, he's actually trying to break into the U.S. Air Force War Operations Plan Response (W.O.P.R.) computer — the machine which controls the country's nuclear missiles. Once he's gained access, David asks the computer to play what he thinks is a video game called Global Thermonuclear War. Much **DRAMATIC TENSION** ensues, but the ending of the film, in which the computer learns that nuclear war is a game that cannot be won by either side is both moving and illuminating.

Wargames contains less than a half hour of actual Seattle footage. About ten minutes into the film, the gratuitous Seattle skyline shot from West Seattle appears, with ferry boats on Elliott Bay and the Space Needle thrown in for good measure. Hey out there, this story in set in Seattle and don't you forget it!

A more specific Seattle sighting occurs in one early scene when David pays a visit to the University of Washington campus to get some help from two of his "hacker" buddies on how he can break into the Protovision programs. Exterior shots place the UW computer hacker department in the Psychology Building on the west side of the main campus.

POWER
(20th Century Fox-1986)

Power is an overly self-righteous story about a ruthless political operative named Pete St. John (Richard Gere), whose only concern is winning elections for his clients and collecting a hefty consultant's fee. His advice to prospective candidates sums up his philosophy. "My job is to get you in. Once you're there, you can do whatever your conscience tells you to do." Another "globetrotting" picture ala **Hit, Power** follows St. John from Latin America to New York, New Mexico to Washington D.C., and Ohio to Seattle as he works his campaign magic for a variety of incumbents and challengers running for various political offices. Apparently, the producers spent only a week filming in Seattle, and it shows.

St. John stops in Seattle twice (for about five minutes each time), to work on the reelection campaign of Governor Andrea Stannard (Michael Learned). The first shot is a ground level view of what else? — the Space Needle — from the corner of Denny Way and Dexter Avenue. Then it's up to the Space Needle Restaurant for a quick "power lunch" with the Governor and her advisors. The next visit to Seattle comes at the Montlake Cut where Governor Stannard is presiding over the opening of boating season. At least, that's the only thing we could come up with to explain the captains hat on her head. One final 30-second scene depicts Governor Stannard chatting with St. John by telephone from the top of a Seattle office building. Did anyone bother to mention to the producers that the capital of Washington State is in Olympia?

THE NUTCRACKER
(Hyperion Pictures-1986)

Seattleites are awfully proud of their local ballet company and its cash cow, **The Nutcracker**. Pairing the timeless story of the Nutcracker with the avant-garde mind of Maurice Sendak was inspired and has made for a Christmas tradition. While filmed in Seattle, this is a one location movie, so unless your Seattle fantasy is the inside of the Opera House, skip it.

the nineties

Above: River Phoenix in **Dogfight,** a movie that successfully substitutes Ballard (!) for mid-sixties SanFrancisco. **Movie Star News.**

Left: Tom Hanks cruises the market in **Sleepless in Seattle,** the ultimate date movie of all time and the scourge of Lesser Seattle. **Tom Reese/Seattle Times**

CLASS OF 1999
(Vestron Pictures-1990)

Cast:	BRADLEY GREGG (Cody Culp), TRACI LIN (Christie Langford), MALCOLM McDOWELL (Miles Langford), STACY KEACH (Dr. Bob Forrest), PATRICK KILPATRICK (Mr. Bryles), PAM GRIER (Ms. Connors), JOHN P. RYAN (Mr. Hardin), DARREN E. BURROWS (Sonny), JOSHUA MILLER (Angel)
Director:	Mark L. Lester
Producer:	Mark L. Lester
Screenplay:	C. Courtney Jones
Music:	Michael Hoenig
Length:	99 minutes
Released:	May 1990
Rated:	Not Rated

Everyone seems to be concerned about the current state of Seattle's public schools. Decaying buildings, gangs, violence, and stressed-out teachers have contributed to an alarming decline in the quality of education provided to students. However, we're not sure if the solution presented in Class of 1999 *is the answer. This futuristic story of a gang-infested Seattle high school that is brutally tamed by a group of robot teachers may seem like a tempting way to regain control over the schools. However, the carnage that's left at the end of this picture when the androids go too far and the students rebel is probably better left on the silver screen.*

Film Synopsis

It's 1999, and portions of many large American cities have been designated as "Free Fire Zones;" urban wastelands populated by heavily-armed thugs. The Seattle Free Fire Zone is controlled by two rival gangs — the Razorheads and the Blackhearts — who have also succeeded in closing down the local high school. Desperate to regain control and educate the students who live in the Zone, school principal Miles Langford (Malcolm McDowell) enlists the help of Dr. Bob Forrest (Stacy Keach) from the Department of Educational Defense.

At a meeting of the school authorities, Dr. Forrest demonstrates a new technology developed by the Megatech Corporation that he promises will help Principal Langford restore normalcy to Kennedy High. The "technology" turns out to be three reconditioned defense department androids who will become high school teachers and give an entirely new meaning to the term "corporal punishment."

One of Kennedy High School's new students is Cody Culp (Bradley Gregg), a Blackheart gang member who has recently been paroled from the state juvenile institution. Despite his sordid past, Cody is determined to go straight and finish school. His brother Angel (Joshua Miller), who is an apprentice Blackheart has another plan. He wants Cody to return to the gang and help them knock off the rival Razorheads and sabotage the reopening of Kennedy High.

Once the new school term begins, however, the Megatech android faculty have other ideas. The first demonstration of their unique approach to classroom control comes in Ms. Connors' (Pam Grier) chemistry class. When a group of rowdy students won't quiet down, Ms. Connors unleashes a barrage of martial arts moves that would make Chuck Norris proud. In Mr. Bryles' (Patrick Kilpatrick) history class, students who misbehave are spanked in front of the other students. While that may seem more humiliating than corporal, a swat from the hand of this robot instructor bruises more than the student's ego.

Disturbed by the robots' behavior, Principal Langford asks Dr. Forrest to terminate the project. The good doctor, however, is not about to cancel a contract for what he sees as a lucrative new market for these cast-off war-surplus androids, and orders the robots to kill Principal Langford. Cody eventually convinces the rival gangs that the teachers are the real enemy, and that they must work together to rid the school of the robots. The final battle scene inside the high school borrows heavily from both **Terminator** films, but the Blackhearts and Razorheads do succeed in sending the androids and Dr. Forrest back to the drawing board.

Seattle People, Places and Things

Class of 1999 was the second film in as many years to use a Seattle public school building as the main setting for its story.

Like **Plain Clothes**, the film used a vacant school building, in this case Lincoln High School in Wallingford. Unlike the generally playful "high school hijinks" film by Martha Coolidge, **Class of 1999** is a high school of horrors, where playful pranks are punished by beatings and executions. Kennedy High is just what you might imagine a public school to be like in the world of Alan Rudolph's **Trouble in Mind.** In fact, Dr. Forrest actually looks a little like Hilly Blue himself, with platinum blonde hair, cataracts, and a portly build.

While the barbed wire, heavily-armed security force, and air-raid sirens do little to enhance the image of Seattle's public schools, the district did permit the film crew to use Lincoln High School for the movie. The Seattle Police Department, however, bristled at the extreme violence in the script, and refused to provide officers to help with the logistics of filming in the city. The King County Sheriffs' office eventually stepped in to assist the production. In contrast, the staff at the Port of Seattle went out of their way to assist the **Class of 1999** filmmakers. A parcel of condemned property just south of Sea-Tac airport was used to film the scenes in the Seattle "Free Fire Zone." In addition, a surplus port building on Harbor Island was blown up as part of the war between the Blackhearts and Razorheads.

Other locations featured in the film include the Four Seasons Olympic Hotel, which is the setting of a dinner meeting between Dr. Forrest and Principal Langford, the parking area underneath the Alaskan Way viaduct which serves as the location for a Blackheart gang party, and the Century Tower Building, which is used for a meeting of the school board and the Department of Educational Defense representatives. There's also a nice chase scene midway through the picture as the robot teachers pursue young Cody on a motorcycle down Western Avenue, past the Pike Place Market, off the Lenora Street "overpass to nowhere," and into the frigid waters of Elliott Bay. Being robots, of course, the teachers simply abandoned their car and walked across the bottom of the bay, eventually emerging in West Seattle directly across from downtown.

The only blooper in the film involves a non-Seattle location. In one of the picture's early scenes, Cody Culp is shown being released from the juvenile institution where he has been incarcerated. In actuality, the scene was filmed at the Washington State Reformatory in Monroe — a state Department of Corrections facility for adults, not juveniles. Neeener, neener. As for cameos, watch for a very young Darren Burrows (Ed from **Northern Exposure**) in the role of Sonny, one of the Blackheart gang members.

What Others Said

"A superior exercise in action and violence [although the film] dissipates into a fantasy world of youth gangs and large collections of unidentified stuntmen who crash through windows on their motorcycles, but serve no other particular purpose."

Roger Ebert

"The paranoid student's dream, full of absurd battle scenes and failed attempts at dark humor."

Vincent Canby, New York Times

"An exciting sequel to **Class of 1984.***"*

Mick Martin

Summary

Like its predecessor **Plain Clothes**, **Class of 1999** is set primarily in one Seattle location (Lincoln High School), and therefore, earns only a middle rating on our scale. Though somewhat sparse, the scenes outside the school are interesting and definitely not run-of-the-mill. Unfortunately, **Class of 1999's** most lasting legacy may be the decision of many Seattle parents to reconsider the viability of private schools.

DOGFIGHT
(Warner Brothers-1991)

Cast:	RIVER PHOENIX (Eddie Birdlace), LILI TAYLOR (Rose Fenney), RICHARD PANEBIANCO (Berzin), ANTHONY CLARK (Okie), MITCHELL WHITFIELD (Benjamin), HOLLY NEAR (Rose Sr.), E.G. DAILY (Marcie)
Director:	Nancy Savoca
Producer:	Peter Newman and Richard Guay
Screenplay:	Bob Comfort
Music:	Mason Daring
Length:	94 minutes
Released:	September 1991
Rated:	R (language, sexual situations)

For years, Seattle suffered from an inferiority complex when it came to comparisons with San Francisco. The California "City by the Bay" was always more cosmopolitan, more naturally beautiful, more stylish — in fact, just a better all-around town than that backwater in the northwest. What sweet revenge then, is the 1991 release Dogfight. The story of a soldier's last few days in the country before shipping out to Vietnam is set in San Francisco during the 1960's, but was filmed on location in Seattle. A cinematic touche´ for the Emerald City.

Film Synopsis

It's 1963, and Eddie Birdlace (River Phoenix) and his marine buddies have just arrived in San Francisco to spend a few days prior to being shipped out to Vietnam. With time to kill and searching for some fun, the soldiers decide to hold a "dogfight" — a contest in which they each chip in $50 to see which of them can bring the ugliest date to a party. The marine whose date is judged to be the ugliest wins the pot.

As the boys fan out through the city in search of their dates, Eddie happens upon an out-of-the-way cafe called Rose's. There, he meets a young waitress named Rose Fenney (Lili Taylor), the daughter of the cafe owner played by Holly Near. Overweight and homely, Rose strikes Eddie as the perfect entry for the dogfight contest. He invites her to a "party" and she agrees to accompany him to a local bar where they will join up with the other "contestants." On the way, however, Eddie realizes that Rose is an intelligent and sweet person, and he guiltily tries to talk her out of going into the bar. Ignorant of the "dogfight" and excited that someone has finally asked her on a date, she insists on going in. When Rose later becomes sick from drinking too much, she finds out about the contest from one of the other girls in the bathroom. Shocked and humiliated, she slaps Eddie and storms out of the bar.

Embarrassed about his actions, Eddie returns to the cafe to makes amends. Sensing his sincerity, she accepts his apology and slowly begins to let him into her world. You see, Rose is deep — really, really deep. She's an aspiring folksinger, with Joan Baez, Odetta and Malvina Reynolds photos carefully pinned on the walls of her bedroom upstairs from the cafe. She is the kind of person who would be angry at Dylan for going electric at the Newport Folk Festival. Her passionate interest in folk and blues music has also made her politically aware. Vietnam has more meaning for her than for Eddie, who thinks he's going to some small country near India. Rose is also more mature and composed, while Eddie seems angry and frustrated at the world and at himself.

Most of the remainder of the movie depicts how Eddie and Rose fall in love. Eventually, Eddie ships off to Vietnam where one of his buddies is killed and he is wounded in battle. When he returns to San Francisco three years later, the streets are populated with flower children and hippies, and Rose's Cafe has turned into a counter-culture coffee house. When Eddie walks in, Rose embraces him trying to ease the painful memories of the war, and the years that have separated them.

Seattle People, Places and Things

Turning modern-day Seattle into San Francisco in the early sixties is no small feat, but is accomplished with surprising realism in **Dogfight**. Although tight shots and primarily evening scenes help to mask the picture's "Seattleness," the filmmakers' ability to transform key Seattle locations into San Francisco references is what ultimately pulls off this urban con job. For example, the Seattle waterfront trolleys double as — guess what? — San Francisco trolleys. You could almost hear the old commercial jingle in the background...."Rice-a-Roni, the San Francisco treat. Ding! Ding!" The Sorrento Hotel (which conveniently has palm trees growing in the front courtyard), plays the role of a posh San Francisco restaurant where Eddie takes Rose to dinner. Even the street sign on the east side of the hotel was changed from Terry to Sacramento Street to further authenticate the location. As in **Frances,** the Paramount Theater is given the Hollywood makeover treatment so that it resembles an early sixties movie palace. The marquee displays the current showing, **The Trouble with Mimi**, a forgettable 1963 release. Seattle's International District was, of course, used for a scene involving San Francisco's Chinatown.

Much of the film's action occurs at Rose's Cafe and the shops nearby. These scenes were filmed on Ballard Avenue — the historic part of the neighborhood that was also featured a few years earlier in **Twice in a Lifetime**. An antique shop currently occupies the storefront that served as Rose's Cafe, with the bay windows that looked into Rose's bedroom above the main floor. Other recognizable locations include City Hall Park and the Kaleenka Cafe on First Avenue. Watch for Peg Phillips of T.V.'s **Northern Exposure** in a cameo role as a customer at Rose's Cafe.

What Others Said

*"**Dogfight** seems to have no clear idea of what these ordinary people are really like. The film wants to be honest (and in its cruelties, it is) but the operative sensibility is that of a sitcom world. The only seemingly spontaneous moment comes at the very end, which is too late."*

Vincent Canby, New York Times

"Even though the premise is incredibly mean-spirited, this is actually a fairly entertaining flick."

Mick Martin

Summary

Like Bob Rafelson's **Black Widow**, a major attraction of **Dogfight** will be the fun of trying to identify what Seattle landmarks were substituted for San Francisco locations in the film. However, **Dogfight** is also a mildly entertaining film, so rent the flick and enjoy the con.

AMERICAN HEART
(Triton Pictures-1992)

Cast:	JEFF BRIDGES (Jack Keely), EDWARD FURLONG (Nick Keely), LUCINDA JENNEY (Charlotte), DON HARVEY (Rainey), TRACEY KAPISKY (Molly), SHAREEN MITCHELL (Diane), CHRISTIAN FRIZZELL (Rollie)
Director:	Martin Bell
Producer:	Roslyn Hellers and Jeff Bridges
Screenplay:	Peter Silverman
Music:	James Newton Howard
Length:	114 minutes
Released:	September 1992
Rating:	R (language, nudity)

A gritty, realistic tale about an ex-con struggling to put the pieces of his shattered life back together, **American Heart** *also provides a depressing glimpse into the underworld of Seattle street kids. Director Martin Bell had come to Seattle in the mid-eighties to shoot* **Streetwise,** *a documentary about street kids which was subsequently nominated for an Oscar. The fictional* **American Heart** *benefits greatly from his earlier filmmaking efforts, which provides a first-hand view of the Seattle that travel agents don't want you to see.*

Film Synopsis

The story begins as convicted burglar Jack Keely (Jeff Bridges) is released from prison and returns to Seattle to try and re-start his life. Unexpectedly, his teenaged son Nick (Edward Furlong, the kid from **Terminator 2**), shows up at the penitentiary and announces that he has run away from his aunt's home where he was living while Dad was in the slammer. While Jack wants no part of parenthood and tries to ditch his son at the bus station, Nick's persistence eventually wears him down and he agrees to let the boy stay on for awhile.

With no money and no immediate job prospects, Jack rents a flophouse in the middle of the city. There's only one mattress, so Jack puts it on the floor for Nick, while he crashes on the innerspring.

(Where is Sunny Kobe Cook when you need her?) Eventually, Jack lands a job as a window-washer, trying to save enough money for his dream of moving to Alaska. After unsuccessfully trying to enroll in the local school, Nick takes a paper route and the two begin a tentative partnership.

Complicating Jack's reintegration into society is Rainey (Don Harvey), his former partner in crime. Although Jack tells Rainey shortly after his release that "my breaking and entering" days are over, Rainey refuses to take no for an answer and ends up stealing Jack's Alaska savings to force him to help out on a burglary job. Jack also tracks down Charlotte (Lucinda Jenney), a world-weary cab driver who had anonymously written to him while he was in prison through the personals column in "American Heart," a magazine for inmates. Unfortunately, their blossoming romance is threatening to Nick and his wish to establish a closer relationship with dad.

As Jack struggles to stay out of trouble, Nick is pretty much left to his own devices and begins to hang out with the local street kids. He soon develops a crush on Molly (Tracey Kapisky), a young hooker who lives downstairs in the same apartment building. To prove his love for her, Nick steals a pair of shoes and when Jack finds out, he kicks Nick out of the house. Out on his own, Nick falls in with Rainey and agrees to work with him on a break-in. Nick brings along his buddy Rollie (Christian Frizell) and when Rollie is accidentally killed, Nick runs away.

When Jack tracks down his son, he tells Nick that they need to leave for Alaska immediately. He sends Nick down to the ferry docks to wait while he tracks down Rainey. Rainey then chases Jack to the waterfront and shoots him just as he boards the boat. As the ferry pulls away from shore, Jack dies in Nick's arms.

Seattle People, Places and Things

Part of what makes **American Heart** such an enjoyable flick from a **Seattle on Film** perspective is director Martin Bell's careful use of Seattle locations and references. For example, in the hands of a director who didn't know any better, Nick might be seen hanging out with the local street kids near the QFC at University Village, instead of outside the parking garage on Yesler Way and near the St. Regis Hotel — places where they actually congregate.

Bell's Seattle references are similarly accurate and appropriate. Jack refers to a jewelry store on "Pill Hill" which Rainey has cased out. In Rainey's apartment is a paper cup from Dag's, the venerable Seattle burger joint which unceremoniously closed it's doors a couple of years ago. In addition, there's plenty of Rainier beer around Jack's house (not much food though), which you'd expect on a window-washer's salary.

Much of the film's action takes place in Jack's seedy apartment building located at 1712 Summit Avenue. Jack and Nick also spend a lot of time down at the piers on the Seattle waterfront dreaming about Alaska, with panoramic views of the city's skyline in the background. Jack, Nick and Charlotte have a typical rainy Seattle picnic at Alki Beach in West Seattle, cooking weenies on a portable gas grill in the back of the car. After Jack boots Nick out of the house, he visits Charlotte at her house in Wallingford to ask for her help. With that view back over Lake Union, you have to wonder how a cab driver like Charlotte could afford the mortgage.

As for other locations, the film features some interesting aerial shots of the city down to Third Avenue behind the old Seattle-First Building. Jack's window washing job takes him inside the then Seattle Trust building, which happened to be vacant during the filming. There are also exterior shots of Jay Jacobs and the old Frederick and Nelson's near Westlake Center. Finally, when Molly needs some extra money, she pays a visit to mom who works as a dancer at the Lusty Lady on First Avenue. Here the viewer is treated to some voyeuristic "interior" shots that were overlooked in previous films like **House of Games** and **Cinderella Liberty**.

What Others Said

"A gritty, well-meaning drama about a father and son on the fringes of society."

Todd McCarthy, Variety

*"**American Heart** benefits greatly from gritty location filming and several memorable performances, especially Jeff Bridges and Edward Furlong."*

Mick Martin

"The relationships do not develop and the narrative is slow-moving and predictable. The writing in particular seems to mistake inarticulateness for authenticity."

Motion Picture Guide

Summary

Here's a picture that's rare among **Seattle on Film** efforts — an excellent story, compelling performances, and carefully chosen locations that enhance the overall effort. While **American Heart's** treatment of the lives of a father and son on the fringes of Seattle society is often depressing, the discriminating viewer with an eye focused beyond the predictability of most movie plots will be greatly rewarded.

In **American Heart**, Jeff Bridges' tour of Seattle's finest living quarters continues at 1712 Summit Avenue. (Private residence, do not disturb.)

SINGLES
(Warner Brothers-1992)

Cast:
CAMPBELL SCOTT (Steve Dunne), KYRA SEDGWICK (Linda Powell), BRIDGET FONDA (Janet Livermore), MATT DILLON (Cliff Poncier), SHEILA KELLY (Debbie Hunt), JIM TRUE (David Bailey), BILL PULLMAN (Dr. Jamison), TOM SKERRITT (Mayor Weber), PETER HORTON (Jamie), ERIC STOLZ (Mime), EDDIE VEDDER, STONE GOSSARD, JEFF AMENT (Seattle rock-dudes), TIM BURTON (Brian), JOHNNY "SUGARBEAR" WILLIS (Rick)

Director: Cameron Crowe
Producer: Cameron Crowe and Richard Hashimoto
Screenplay: Cameron Crowe
Music: Paul Westerberg
Length: 99 minutes
Released: October 1992
Rating: PG-13 (sexual situations, language)

*The second feature film from rock writer turned director Cameron Crowe, **Singles** provides a glimpse into the Seattle grunge music sub-culture of the early 1990's. While the movie is a bit of an angst-ridden relationship potboiler, it effectively captures a moment when Seattle rode to the front of the national music scene.*

Film Synopsis

The rather thin plot concerns the romantic relationships of a group of young, "20-something" singles living in the same Capitol Hill apartment building. Steve Dunne (Campbell Scott) is a planner with the state Department of Transportation who wants to launch a high-speed commuter rail system in the Seattle area. He soon falls for Linda Powell (Kyra Sedgwick), an activist with the "Seattle Environmental Council" who is living by herself and proud of it. During the ensuing hour and a half, they fall in love, break-up and reconcile, while spouting such sappy lines as, "I'm tired of all the games," "You always say the perfect thing," and "I miss albums." We wish we were in touch with our feelings as much as these two whiners.

The other major romantic subplot concerns Janet Livermore (Bridget Fonda) and Cliff Poncier (Matt Dillon), two employees of a local coffee house called The Java Stop. Cliff is also a part-time artist and the lead singer of a local underground rock band called Citizen Dick. Janet is hopelessly infatuated with Cliff who of course, barely notices her. In desperation for some minor sign of affection, she even goes so far as scheduling breast enlargement surgery in the hopes of awakening his romantic interest. When she finally wises up and dumps him, he does a compete about face, and realizes that he: (a) had taken her for granted; (b) didn't know what he had when he had it and; (c) didn't know how lucky he was........and so on and so on. Unfortunately, they reconcile as well.

The film does excel in small recurring references that define dating and relationships in the early 1990's. For example, a true sign of romantic commitment is giving your partner their own remote control for your garage door opener. Real, normal guys are constantly compared to "Mr. Sensitive Ponytail Man." One scene takes place at a "safe sex" party where revelers are dressed as their favorite contraceptive. While these references will probably seem hopelessly dated in a few years, they are witty cultural mileposts.

Seattle People, Places and Things

Like a 1990's version of the introductory scenes to **The Slender Thread**, **Singles** opens with an extended panoramic montage of the downtown Seattle skyline at night, the Space Needle, ferry boats on Elliott Bay, the Pike Place Market, the Neptune Theater and the venerable Wallingford Food Giant — a loving portrait of a city that is vibrant and alive. Unlike many films scripted by L.A. "hacks," **Singles** delves deep into Seattle and gets its references right. Cameron Crowe is now a local (and married to Heart's Nancy Wilson), and it shows.

Much of the action takes place at the aforementioned Java Stop — a funky, seedy coffee house that is in reality the O.K. Hotel, a funky, seedy, alternative music club. The other major gathering point in the film is the singles apartment complex, which are the Coryell Apartments on East Thomas Avenue, about two blocks from Group Health Hospital. Other scenes were filmed at Gasworks Park, the Virginia Inn and Pioneer Square.

Because Crowe is a local, typical bloopers were hard to find. The film is sprinkled with precise Seattle references ("Where do you want to eat, Costas or the 321?). In one early scene, Linda corrects a prospective beau who has referred to the UW as the U-"Double U" as opposed to the more locally correct U-"Dub." Nevertheless, we were able to spot a couple of regional miscues. For example, Steve's bright and airy cubicle at the Department of Transportation (DOT) is large enough for the Sonics to hold a half-court scrimmage. In reality, a junior staffer at DOT would be lucky to get nine square feet in a windowless basement. Later, when Steve is pitching his high-speed commuter rail project to Mayor Weber (Tom Skerritt in a cameo preview of his political future?), Hizzoner rejects the idea outright. Now, most us know that no Seattle mayor would be able to make a decision like that so quickly and decisively. In Our City of Perpetual Consensus, we'd need to appoint two or three commissions just to decide what to order for lunch.

Much of what gives **Singles** it's unique tone and style is the liberal dose of music cameos. For example, Eddie Vedder, Jeff Ament and Stone Gossard from Pearl Jam appear as three-quarters of Citizen Dick, Cliff Poncier's aspiring local grunge rock band. At the time **Singles** was made, Pearl Jam was on the verge of its commercial breakthrough. Now it's hard to imagine them with the time, desire, or sense of humor to play these roles. Bruce Pavitt, the founder of Sub Pop Records also appears, as does Chris Cornell from Soundgarden and Pat DiNizio of The Smithereens. DiNizio was apparently so underwhelmed by his experience that he later penned a song entitled, "Sick of Seattle." Finally, in a nod to Seattle's musical past, Jimi Hendrix's grave appears as itself.

A few other non-musical cameos are worth noting. During Steve and Linda's first romantic tryst, Xavier McDaniel and Wayne Cody (remember them?), hold a post-game interview which turns into a sexual admonition for Steve. If Xavier's game had been as solid as his advice, he might still be a Sonic today. In addition, Eric Stolz appears as a street-performing mime, Peter Horton (from **Thirtysomething**) plays Debbie Hunt's video dating boyfriend, and director Tim Burton (**Beetlejuice, Batman,** and **The Nightmare Before Christmas**) appears as the director of a video dating service, referring to himself as the next "Martin Scorseeeeez!"

What Others Said

"Crowe [is] a filmmaker with an uncanny ear for the ways in which humorous, vastly likeable young characters might express themselves, with a jokey casualness that's a lot more substantial than it sounds."

Janet Maslin, New York Times

"Crowe has a definite ear for the verbal byplay of young love, and his ensemble cast is superb."

Mick Martin

Summary

Singles shows Cameron Crowe to be an enduring presence in movie making. As long as he stays in the local area, we're likely to be treated to more wonderful celluloid time capsules. So rent the movie, ignore the plot, and enjoy the "scene."

Single in Seattle? The Coryell Apartments await your first and last month's rent and cleaning deposit. (Private residence, do not disturb). Unless, of course you can join the tasteful houseboat navy of . . . . . .

SLEEPLESS IN SEATTLE
(Tri-Star/Sony-1993)

Cast:
: TOM HANKS (Sam Baldwin), MEG RYAN (Annie Reed), ROSS MALINGER (Jonah Baldwin), ROSIE O'DONNELL (Becky), ROB REINER (Jay) RITA WILSON (Suzy), CAREY LOWELL (Maggie Baldwin), BILL PULLMAN (Walter), BARBARA GARRICK (Victoria), DAVID HYDE PIERCE (Dennis Reed), BRIAN McCONNACHIE (Bob)

Director: Nora Ephron
Producer: Gary Foster
Screenplay: Nora Ephron, David S. Ward and Jeff Arch
Music: Marc Shaiman
Length: 100 minutes
Released: June 1993
Rating: PG (adult situations)

A strong contender for the top-ten all time "date movies" list, **Sleepless in Seattle** *firmly established Tom Hanks as a Hollywood superstar, and created a new national awareness of Seattle and Seattle filmmaking. Part tearjerker, part screwball comedy,* **Sleepless in Seattle** *preaches faith in the virtues of romance and the principle that the right person is out there — even if it takes the modern miracle of talk radio to find them.*

Film Synopsis

Sam Baldwin (Tom Hanks) is a recently widowed architect living in Chicago with his son Jonah (Ross Malinger). Depressed, he decides to move to Seattle to begin his life again. He settles into a comfortable Westlake houseboat, but still finds it hard to shake the memory of his wife, Maggie (played in flashbacks by Carey Lowell).

Jonah (the designated child whois wiser than his parents), decides at Christmas that it's time for dad to stop grieving, and calls a national talk radio psychologist for help. Jonah deftly maneuvers his dad to the phone, where the "talk doc" gets him to begin to open up, dubbing him "Sleepless in Seattle" in the process. Women across the country melt for "Sleepless," and the marriage proposals begin to flood in through the mail.

One listener is Annie Reed (Meg Ryan), a reporter for the Baltimore Sun who is engaged to be married to a perfectly nice but perfectly boring man named Walter (Bill Pullman). She is fascinated by Sam's heartfelt description of his late wife and their marriage, but rather than taking the direct approach, she pitches a story idea to her editors to allow her to track down Sleepless.

After getting leads and photographs from a private investigator, Annie jets off to Seattle, where she tries to introduce herself to Sam, but can't quite muster the nerve. Instead she tracks him through Seattle, becoming thoroughly charmed by his essential "SNAG-ness" (that's Sensitive New-Age Guy). When she finally steels herself to approach him, she sees Sam in the embrace of another woman, who is actually his sister.

The remainder of the film is a "will she/won't she" exercise, as we wait to see whether Sam and Annie will connect. The climax revolves around a planned meeting at the Empire State Building on Valentine's Day, arranged long distance by Jonah. (Sam is sure lucky to have Jonah around — left to his own devices he would still be placing personals ads in The Stranger). At the end "will she/won't she" turns to "she does" (remember, this is a date movie), and hearts melt all around as Jimmy Durante croons into the moonlight.

The plot of **Sleepless in Seattle** is rather silly and contrived, but it does have some wonderful observational moments about modern life and the dating scene. When Sam finally decides to begin dating again, he executes a hilarious hesitation dance with the phone, while the soundtrack plays Gene Autry's "Back in the Saddle Again." Also, there is a funny discussion of why some films are "chick flicks" — and this is one — launching that term into common usage.

Seattle People, Places and Things

While Seattle is featured in the title, the city appears in only about a third of the movie. But what a third — the local visitor's bureau couldn't have asked for a better portrayal of (all together now), THE MOST LIVABLE CITY IN AMERICA!

Sam and Jonah's houseboat is located in a marina at 2460 Westlake Avenue, and you get a real feel for the Seattle houseboat experience (at least the upscale kind). Later, there is an extended sequence with Sam and his contractor friend Jay (played by Rob Reiner — keeping his acting chops up in case he makes more dogs like **North**), taking an extended walk up First Avenue, turning down Pine Street, past the Inn at the Market and on down to the Pike Place Market. They have lunch at the horseshoe counter of the Athenian Inn, drinking what appear to be authentic microbrews.

Sea-Tac airport makes its obligatory **Seattle on Film** appearance about halfway through the movie, as does the Space Needle in a full shot from Western Avenue. There is also a shot to Gasworks Park from the water, and a long sequence in which Annie tracks Sam and Jonah from the houseboat, across the Fremont Bridge, to Alki. This is the film's most notorious blooper. Let's see now. Sam and Jonah leave the houseboat on Lake Union in a two-person, four-horsepower outboard boat, and end up at Alki Beach, with Annie, who has never been to Seattle, trailing them in a car by driving north over the Fremont Bridge. Sure.

Another seasonal blooper has Sam peering off his houseboat toward Gasworks on New Year's Eve and seeing a fireworks display to rival the greatest of Ivar's Fourth of July fests. There is also a reference to a "man of the year in Seattle Magazine" which would be fine, except there was no Seattle Magazine at the time the film was shot. The subsequent revival of the magazine was no doubt financed by the filmmakers to invalidate this blooper.

At the end of the film, when Meg Ryan goes to the top of the Empire State Building (scenes that were filmed inside a makeshift soundstage at the Sand Point Naval Air Station), she finds it empty — Sam and Jonah are gone. She is about to do the same when she notices a Seattle Mariners sports bag that Jonah has left behind. When Jonah comes back to retrieve his bag (which hardly seems worth it, considering the team's record of futility), Cupid finally gets to let loose his arrow.

Sleepless in Seattle required moviemakers to dip into their bag of tricks. While set at Christmastime, the film was actually shot during the summer of 1992. This required that the landscape around the Lake Union houseboat community be stripped of its summer foliage and replaced with evergreens, wreaths, and Christmas lights. During the Pike Place scenes, the cast and extras had to wear winter garb, even though the temperature was approaching the 90's. The result was a movie that convincingly portrayed the Seattle winter (except for those darn fireworks).

What Others Said

"As ephemeral as a talk show, as contrived as the late show, and yet so warm and gentle I smiled the whole way through."

Roger Ebert

*"Not since 'Love Story' has there been such a movie that so shrewdly and predictably manipulated the emotions for such entertaining effect. Be warned, though: **Sleepless in Seattle** is a movie you may hate yourself in the morning for having loved the night before."*

Vincent Canby, New York Times

Summary

Sleepless in Seattle is best experienced as a slick and funny romance — the perfect date movie and an all-time, top-ten "chick flick."

Mi Casa es su casa at 2460 Westlake. (Private residence, do not disturb.)

THE VANISHING
(20th Century Fox -1993)

Cast:	JEFF BRIDGES (Barney Cousins), KIEFER SUTHERLAND (Jeff Harriman), NANCY TRAVIS (Rita), SANDRA BULLOCK (Diane Shaver), PARK OVERALL (Lynn), MAGGIE LINDERMAN (Denise Cousins), LISA EICHHORN (Helene)
Director:	George Sluizer
Producer:	Larry Brezner and Paul Schiff
Screenplay:	Todd Graff
Music:	Jerry Goldsmith
Length:	110 minutes
Released:	November 1993
Rating:	R (language, subject matter)

During the summer of 1974, women in the Seattle area were terrified by reports of a young man named Ted, who was kidnapping and murdering young women by feigning a broken arm and asking for help with his boat. The similarities of this tragic episode to the film **The Vanishing** *are really too close for comfort. An outwardly normal chemistry professor practices his abduction techniques by faking a bum arm, pretending to have car trouble, and then ultimately acting on his psychopathic impulses. Not a film for the easily unsettled.*

Film Synopsis

It's 1989, and Barney Cousins (Jeff Bridges) is holed-up in his remote vacation cabin practicing to kidnap and murder an unsuspecting victim. A college chemistry instructor who is married and has a beautiful young daughter, Barney appears normal but is obviously one sick puppy. The scene then shifts to Jeff Harriman (Kiefer Sutherland) and his girlfriend Diane Shaver (Sandra Bullock), who are driving together through the Cascade mountains. When they pull over at a truck stop, Diane goes into the store to buy something to eat but fails to return to the car. Jeff frantically searches the area but to no avail. Diane has vanished into thin air.

Three years later, Jeff is still obsessed with finding Diane. Plastering her picture on every billboard in the city and appearing on local talkshows, he has become something of a minor celebrity. Still, his inability to discover the cause of her disappearance torments Jeff, and he wanders the countryside desperately looking for clues. One night he stops in a roadside diner and meets Rita (Nancy Travis), a beautiful waitress who falls for this tortured soul nursing a cup of coffee at the counter. Eventually, they fall in love and move into an apartment together.

Despite his promise to Rita that he has put his obsession with finding his old girlfriend behind him, Jeff continues to secretly search for Diane. When Rita discovers his deception, she walks out, just as Barney Cousins appears on the scene to make a proposition. If Jeff will agree to experience exactly what Diane did, he will find out what happened to her. Reluctantly, he accompanies Barney to the truck stop where Diane vanished three years ago, and drinks some coffee that Barney has drugged. When he comes to, he is trapped inside a small wooden box which has been buried on the grounds of Barney's cabin, and at that moment realizes that Diane had met the same fate.

Now in the original 1988 Dutch version, this is where the picture ends — bleak, chilling and haunting. But hey, this is Hollywood and Americans simply won't flock in droves to see a film with an ending like that. Therefore, enter lovely Rita at the proverbial eleventh hour. She tracks down Barney's address from the license plate number that was noticed by a neighbor, and arrives at the cabin just in time to rescue the unconscious Jeff, and help ensure that Barney gets his in the end,

Seattle People, Places and Things

The Vanishing has much to offer the Seattle on Film fan, particularly its ability to provide a fresh look at some long overused location shots. For example, Jeff and Diane's apartment, which is located in a small complex on the corner of Second Avenue North and Aloha Street on the south slope of Queen Anne Hill, provides numerous views of the Space Needle. The use of some creative camera angles both from inside and outside the apartment provides the illusion that the Needle is both close to and far away from the residence. This makes it hard for even the most experienced Seattle-filmwatchers to precisely determine the apartment's location.

Similarly, the shots east along Aloha Street toward Lake Union and Aurora Avenue are tightly framed, providing scant clue that the neighborhood in the background is actually Capitol Hill. While these features might not sound impressive to you, **The Vanishing** was actually one of the last movies we watched while writing this book. We can guarantee you that after sitting through 40 movies filled with gratuitous shots of Space Needles, ferry boats, and the Pike Place Market, we were ready to acclaim any film that made identifying Seattle locations even remotely challenging.

Other featured landmarks include the Seattle Yacht Club, the Metro bus tunnel, Yesler Avenue looking west towards Pioneer Square and the Alaskan Way viaduct, the Fantasy Unlimited store at First Avenue and Pike Street, and Eastlake Avenue directly below the I-5 Ship Canal bridge. The KIRO Channel 7 news team also makes a cameo appearance.

For longtime Seattlelites, the film's most unsettling moments come about two-thirds of the way through the picture, as Barney tells Jeff how he rehearsed Diane's abduction. He first puts a fake cast on his arm and then pretends to have trouble starting his car. He actually manages to get one woman into the car with him, when she sees a picture of his wife and daughter and figures Barney for a stable family man. When that abduction attempt goes awry, he gives up hope until he accidently runs into Diane in the truck stop store. As we mentioned before, the parallels to the Ted Bundy story are chillingly similar.

While **The Vanishing** is thankfully devoid of obvious bloopers, the constant use of "drugged" coffee does nothing to enhance the city's reputation as the "Koffee Kingdom." Somehow we can't imagine people knocking back a tall, skinny decaf with a double darvon.

What Others Said

"The **Vanishing** *suffers from an imbalance caused by an overemphasis on the sociopathic killer played by Jeff Bridges. The everyman point of view of the original, which gave it a highly unsettled quality, has been replaced by a concentration on the methods used by Bridges to lure women into his car."*

Mick Martin

*The first three-fourths of the film are suitably intriguing,
faithfully transplanting the original story to a Seattle setting.
But at this point, one can almost hear the echoes of a
Hollywood exec saying, "You know what this film needs?" The
"Vanishing" of the title could refer to the film's carefully-
constructed characterizations, which evaporate at the start of
the last reel, to be replaced by all the standard Hollywood
gimmicks and tricks, guaranteeing to turn any "art house film"
into a viable commodity.*

Craig Boldman, Critics' Choice

Summary

Although most film critics prefer its 1988 European predecessor,
The Vanishing is still a compelling thriller. The picture's relatively
fresh approach to showcasing its Seattle scenes will also appeal to
the most intrepid Seattle film sleuths.

Jeff and Diane's Queen Anne apartment at the corner of Second
Avenue North and Aloha. A bit more spacious than the
accomodations Barney Cousins offered Jeff. (Private residence, do
not disturb)

LITTLE BUDDHA
(Ciby 2000-1994)

Cast:	CHRIS ISAAK (Dean Conrad), BRIDGET FONDA (Lisa Conrad), KEANU REEVES (Prince Siddhartha), YING RUOCHENG (Lama Norbu), ALEX WISENDANGER (Jesse Conrad), RAJU LAI (Raju), GREISHMA MAKAR SINGH (Gita), GESHE TSULTIN GYELSEN (Lama Dorje)
Director:	Bernardo Bertolucci
Producer:	Jeremy Thomas
Screenplay:	Mark Peploe and Rudy Wurlitzer
Music:	Ryuichi Sakamoto
Length:	120 minutes
Released:	June 1994
Rating:	PG (subject matter)

Little Buddha is the story of the reincarnation of a Tibetan holy man who may be living in the body of a young Seattle boy. The film represents several "firsts." It was renowned movie director Bernardo Bertolucci's first film shot in the United States, and the first major Seattle picture to deal with the subject of religion and spirituality. Little Buddha was also the premiere attraction at the 20th Seattle International Film Festival, held in May 1994.

Film Synopsis

An elderly Buddhist monk named Lama Norbu (Ying Ruocheng) is instructing his young disciples at a monastery in Bhutan, when a mysterious telegram arrives. The message indicates that Tibetan monks in Seattle think they have finally found the reincarnation of a beloved lama in the body of a young Seattle boy named Jesse Conrad (Alex Wiesendanger). Eager to determine if the claim is true, Lama Norbu hops a plane to Seattle, meets the other monks at the airport, and heads straight for the young boy's house.

When they arrive, they are greeted by Jesse's mother Lisa (Bridget Fonda). Unfazed by the strange visitors, she invites the monks into the house. When husband Dean (Chris Isaak) arrives home, the monks proceed to tell the Conrads that they believe their son is the reincarnation of their dear friend and teacher who passed away nine years ago. Oh, and by the way, they'd like to take Jesse back to Bhutan just to make sure. While not consenting immediately to the proposition, the Conrad's allow the monks to leave Jesse with a storybook about the early life of the Buddha, and promise to let them visit with him again.

Now why do some of these recent theatrical releases make Seattlelites look so naive and gullible? First, the Hendersons bring home an eight foot sasquatch who proceeds to clumsily rip their home to shreds. Then, in **The Hand That Rocks the Cradle**, the Bartels hire a nanny without references who turns out to be a psychotic murderer. Now the Conrads entertain the idea of letting a group of Buddhist monks take their son back to a monastery in Bhutan, to see if he might be the reincarnation of a deceased holy man. Next thing you know, they'll imply that we're a bunch of rubes who would be stupid enough to sell millions of bonds to unsuspecting investors for a bunch of nuclear power plants we don't really need. Oh, you heard about that one.

At this point, the story begins to move back and forth among four locations: Seattle, Bhutan, Kathmandu and ancient India. As young Jesse reads the picture book given to him by the monks, we are told the story of Prince Siddhartha (Keanu Reeves); the legendary figure from ancient India who rejected his life of wealth and comfort in order to search for the true meaning of life, eventually becoming the Buddha, or "The Enlightened One." Despite Mr. Reeves' heavy makeup, long braided hair, and British-Indian accent, it's awfully hard to keep from viewing this part of the picture without conjuring up the image of **Buddha and Ted's Excellent Adventure**.

In between scenes of Prince Siddhartha's life, the film also continues the story of young Jesse, his growing fondness for the monks, and the transformation of his parents from cautious skeptics to willing participants in what will become a spiritual transformation for all of them. Following the suicide of his business partner, Dean decides to accompany Jesse back to Nepal and Bhutan with Lama Norbu and the other monks. When they arrive, the Conrads discover that there are two other children who are also thought to be the reincarnation of the lama.

While the three candidates are watched closely by the monks for signs that one of them may be the true reincarnation, the story of Prince Siddhartha and his transformation to The Buddha is completed. Finally, it is left to Lama Norbu to make the final choice between the three children. In a decision that would have made Congress proud, he claims that each of them possesses an equal portion of the spirit of the deceased holy man. After Lama Norbu dies, each child receives a portion of his ashes which the Conrad's scatter into the waters of Elliott Bay as the film ends.

Seattle People, Places and Things

As mentioned above, **Little Buddha** is a film that is divided among four locations: Seattle, modern-day Nepal and Bhutan, and ancient India. The question on our minds when we saw this film was why Seattle? The reincarnation of the lama could just have easily been in the body of any small boy from anytown U.S.A. Why not San Francisco, Boston or Racine? The answer was provided by the master director himself in an interview with The Weekly shortly after the film opened. Bertolucci said that he chose Seattle as the film's location because the city provided a stark contrast to the burnished yellow scenes of ancient India. Seattle, he thought, fit the bill extremely well — a modern, secular city with an admirable mix of old and new architecture, as well as a cold Northwest light that came through on film.

Although the Seattle scenes in **Little Buddha** comprise only about one-third of the total movie, they are beautifully photographed. The Conrad home is located on the corner of Sixth Avenue West and Prospect, on the south slope of Queen Anne Hill. The ultra-modern structure provides magnificent views of the city, the Space Needle, Elliott Bay and the Cascade mountains in both day and evening wear. After learning of the death of his business partner, Dean Conrad pulls his car over to the side of the Yesler Way I-5 overpass, staring back at the Smith Tower. In the film's final scene, the Conrad family scatters the ashes of Lama Norbu into the waters of Elliott Bay as the sunset reflects off the downtown skyline and then disappears slowly over the Olympic Mountains.

Now Tibetan monks in Seattle are not a very common sight, which does make for some peculiar scenes. Heading into Seattle from the airport, the monks proceed north on I-5, then segue onto the Alaskan Way viaduct while country music blares from the radio. The local Buddhist temple scenes were filmed at the Sakya Monastery on Phinney Ridge near Woodland Park.   Later, the movie monks can be seen wandering through the Seattle Art Museum so little Jesse can show them a statute of the Buddha. Finally, in an homage to Seattle movies of the past, the monks insist on taking a monorail ride, presumably to retrace the historic path of Elvis and little Sue Lin in **It Happened at the World's Fair** more than 30 years earlier. This leads to the question of why the monks weren't more preoccupied with searching the world for the reincarnation of Elvis, since he ended up looking a lot like a Buddha himself in later years.

Now you might think a master director like Bernardo Bertolucci would have gone to great lengths to avoid any careless local bloopers in such a serious picture. You'd think that, but you would be wrong. When Jesse finally arrives in Tibet, for the first time we see him wearing a baseball cap. An Oakland A's cap! Now we know they're perpetually terrible, and they play indoors during the 50 days each year that the weather is really nice, but hey, they're OUR crummy baseball team, and if you're going to make a movie about a nine-year old Seattle boy who travels 4,500 miles away from home, chances are he's going to be wearing his Mariners cap. Even some shots of a Ken Griffey Jr. poster in Jesse's room can't make-up for this unforgivable omission.

Another local blooper involves the small boat that the Conrad family takes out onto Elliott Bay in the film's final scene. Clearly displayed on the stern is the boat's name — the Mary Jane — and its homeport of Tacoma, Washington. Tacoma. Yeah, we guess it was probably pretty hard to find just the right kind of boat in Seattle. Maybe Tacoma has more "spiritual" watercraft.

What Others Said

"You can't help feeling that the monks struck lucky: the child they seek just happens to live in a hip city, in the bosom of a family unfazed by alternative religions, in a house that contrasts nicely with the warm tones of the monks' own living space back in Bhutan. Think how tricky it could have been if the

Seattle on Film

vision had led them to, say, an unemployed sheet metal worker in Detroit — someone who isn't so happy to find a bunch of smilers in full-length saffron standing on his doorstep and asking if they could borrow his son."

Anthony Lane, The New Yorker

"After 30 years of making passionately skeptical movies, Bertolucci has made a film of the most sophisticated simplicity. His triumph is to make you see the Buddhist world through his eyes. It shines like innocence reincarnated."

Richard Corliss, Time

Summary

Despite not being his best work, **Little Buddha** is still a Bernardo Bertolucci picture shot right here in our own backyard, making it a must-see for anyone who purports to call themselves a film buff.

Looming over the sidewalk at Sixth and Prospect, the house of the young Buddha awaits. (Private residence, do not disturb)

DISCLOSURE
(Warner Brothers-1994)

Cast:	MICHAEL DOUGLAS (Tom Sanders), DEMI MOORE (Meredith Johnson), DONALD SUTHERLAND (Bob Garvin), CAROLINE GOODALL (Susan Hendler), ROMA MAFFIA (Catherine Alvarez), NICHOLAS SADLER (Don Cherry), DENNIS MILLER (Mark Lewyn)
Director:	Barry Levinson
Producer:	Barry Levinson and Michael Crichton
Screenplay:	Paul Attanasio (based on the book by Michael Crichton)
Music:	Ennio Morricone
Length:	128 minutes
Released:	December 1994
Rating:	R (sexual situations, language)

Hot-city, hot-director, and hot-writer combined to produce this cautionary melodrama for the '90s — a male computer industry executive sexually harassed and set-up by his aggressive female boss. While the movie could have been shot anywhere, Seattle's high-tech reputation makes it a believable locale for this Hollywood eye-candy.

Film Synopsis

Tom Sanders (Michael Douglas) is a key executive at the Seattle office of DigiCom, a high-flying computer firm. Sanders is about to hit the jackpot, as a pending merger turns his stock options into gold and he gets a lucrative promotion.

His life quicky unravels when he is passed over for the promotion, which goes to beautiful Meredith Johnson (Demi Moore), a California-based protege of DigiCom founder Bob Garvin (Donald Sutherland) and a former lover of Sanders'. At the end of her first day, Johnson invites Sanders to her office to discuss old times, whereupon she promptly tries to jump his bones. Sanders ultimately rejects her, only to find the next day that she has accused him of sexual harassment.

Sanders fights back, only to find that management has closed ranks around Johnson, and that a key project of his may have been sabotaged. Sanders hires a tough, flamboyant attorney named Catherine Alvarez (Roma Maffia), but soon finds out that the sexual harassment charge is just part of a larger, more devious puzzle.

Anonymous e-mail advice from an ally, and a trip into virtual reality ultimately give Sanders the ammunition he needs to vindicate himself and save his job.

Seattle People, Places and Things

Much of the action in the film occurs in the DigiCom offices, which appear to be a typical Pioneer Square complex of exposed brick, fine woods, and much glass. Actually, these scenes were filmed on the Warner Brothers lot in Burbank, with the cast and crew moving to Seattle after ten weeks of shooting.

The Seattle scenes are essentially a postcard of tourist favorites. Since Sanders and family live on Bainbridge Island we get ferries, ferries and more ferries. DigiCom itself is located in Pioneer Square but we never get much of a feel for the area. There are also some beautiful shots of the Arboretum, the Pike Place Market, and the Metro bus tunnel. The Four Seasons Olympic — Seattle's official movie hotel — makes a brief appearance as well. One authentic touch locates the offices of the scrappy sexual harassment attorney in the Smith Tower. A jarring note for locals occurs early when Sanders begins his day with a nice cup of tea. Tea? Maybe we'd better sell those Starbucks shares.

Disclosure also tends to reinforce Seattle's fear of "Californication." DigiCom is a Silicon Valley firm, and the head office employees are portayed as ruthless and corrupt. In Tinseltown's view, local employees just can't quite play business hardball (even with a retractable roof stadium).

Comedian Dennis Miller has a small, but key role, as one of DigiCom's hotshot programmers, and he appears to have improvised most of his cutting one-liners. Miller's east coast edge is far from Seattle mellow, but it livens up the movie until he is called on to really act in a confrontation with Sanders at a swank charity gala. To review Miller's performance with one of his own lines, he has as much range as a Daisy air rifle.

What Others Said

"Michael Douglas is passed over for a coveted senior post in his <u>San Francisco</u> computer firm, and it is given to his former lover of a decade earlier, played by Demi Moore." (And they say that Americans don't know anything about geography!)

The London Times

"What's legitimately disturbing about **Disclosure** *is its utter confusion of technology and eroticism. The computer-age products in this film easily eclipse the human players, and the sex appeal of ingenious engineering is everywhere.*

Janet Maslin, New York Times

Summary

Not a first tier offering on either the fine film or **Seattle on Film** scales, **Disclosure** is best enjoyed as a big-studio, big-star diversion that won't tax your brain cells.

MAD LOVE
(Touchstone Pictures - 1995)

Cast:	CHRIS O'DONNELL (Matt Leland), DREW BARRYMORE (Casey Roberts), JOAN ALLEN (Margaret Roberts), KEVIN DUNN (Clifford Leland), JUDE CICCOLELLA (Richard Roberts)
Director:	Antonia Bird
Producer:	David Manson
Screenplay:	Paula Milne
Music:	Andy Roberts
Length:	99 minutes
Released:	May 1995
Rating:	PG-13 (sexual situations)

All of us went to high school with classmates who represented the extremes of the typical high school social types. There were straight arrow kids who got straight A's and went to colleges in the East. There were rebellious kids who smoked, took drugs and also went to colleges in the East. The rest of us average types hung out and went to the UW. Do you ever remember kids from these two different groups falling in love? Neither do we, although Hollywood seems to think that most teenagers are secure enough in themselves to date against type. **Mad Love** *much like its* **Seattle on Film** *predecessor* **Say Anything** *once again proves that filmmakers would rather deal with the "what could be" rather than the "what is."*

Film Synopsis

Casey Roberts (Drew Barrymore) and Matt Leland (Chris O'Donnell) are high school students in Seattle. Matt is a straight-A student who's hyper-responsible and headed for marriage, two kids, a mortgage in Bellevue and an ulcer by forty. Casey is wild, unpredictable, and slightly suicidal -- your basic "Courtney Love-in-training" who will do anything to shock or upset the status quo. One night while stargazing through his telescope, Matt spots Casey jet skiing in the middle of the night on Lake Washington. Of course, it's love at first sight (at least what he could see in the dark), and the two begin a tentative courtship.

While romance blooms between Casey and Matt, relationships with their parents begin to deteriorate. Mr. Leland (Kevin Dunn), who's wife abandoned the family when Matt was nine, has come to depend on his eldest son to take care of his younger brother and sister, and begins to resent the extra time that Matt is spending with his new girlfriend. Casey's parents on the other hand are control freaks, particularly her father who is a UW art professor. When she pulls the school fire alarm one day to get Matt's attention, Dad decides to ground her and forbids her from seeing Matt. Upset and enraged, she dives into the lake outside her house. Unbeknownest to her, Matt has watched the whole scene through his telescope and dives into the lake, believing he is foiling a suicide attempt.

Mr. Roberts (vying for Father of the Year honors), then decides to commit Casey to a local mental health treatment center. Matt proceeds to break her out of the facility and the two embark on a southwestern roadtrip. Although their freedom is intoxicating for a short time, Matt is eventually unable to cope with Casey's instability and phones home to ask her mom for help. Casey and Matt end up returning to Seattle to get her the help she finally feels she needs.

Seattle People, Places and Things

Mad Love is a picture that tries just "a wee bit too hard" to be a Seattle flick. Did director Antonia Bird get an advance copy of our manuscript so she would be sure not to miss any of the **Seattle on Film** landmarks? I mean we've got Elliott Bay, the ferries, we've got the Alaskan Way viaduct, the waterfront, the Pike Place Market and the downtown skyline. What, no Ballard? And how about those traditional Seattle adolescent pasttimes? When school let's out, there's nothing Matt and his friends like better than to hop downtown for a cup of java and a biscotti. Huh? Don't teenagers go home after school and pork-out on nachos anymore?

Cameos are plentiful in **Mad Love**. Elaine Miles (Marilyn from **Northern Exposure**) has a bit part as the Roberts' housekeeper, played with the same dramatic range she displayed for five years on CBS. "Uh, huh. Nope. Not here." Could be Oscar time! Matt's little siblings are seen watching **Bill Nye the Science Guy** on Channel 9 as Bill yells out his signature line "Science Rules!"

Early on in the flick as the Leland family prepares to leave the house for the day, Rich Marriott, KING's No. 2 weather guy delivers the day's forecast. Later, when Matt is alone in his room at night, the reflection of the T.V. screen can be seen through his bedroom window with — guess who? — Marriott again, delivering the evening weather report. This guy doesn't get this much airtime on Channel 5!

The film also features a couple of good bloopers. When referring to her Dad's job, Casey mentions that he's a professor a the "U-Double-U." And where might that school be little lady? Even more unbelievable is the Roberts' house, an ultra-modern edifice on the shores of Lake Washington. With three levels and about 4,000 square feet, we've gotta be talking $1 million purchase price. Now, as an art professor at the UW, Mr. Roberts is probably pulling down just enough bread to afford a three-bedroom, non-view house in the Maple Leaf neighborhood. Maybe he bought Microsoft at 20.

What Others Said

*"If **Mad Love** does a better job than many Hollywood movies at maintaining a level-headed psychological credibility, this story of young lovers who impulsively flee their middle class backgrounds still comes in a thick romantic mist."*

Stephen Holden, New York Times

*"Littered with unbuttoned flannel shirts and matted hair, **Mad Love** aspires to be a sexy and sleek reflection of pop culture. Unfortunately, only its energy-infused soundtrack — a veritable who's who of alternative rock — succeeds, stranding the rest of the film at the opening credits."*

Tom Meek, Critic's Choice

Summary

Mad Love is a moderately enjoyable flick -- perfect for the bargain night rentals. O.K., so maybe we're just grumpy because we didn't recognize much of the soundtrack music, proving what out-of-touch, middle-aged graybeards we have become. Tragic.

The Rest of the Nineties (so far)

GHOST DAD
(Universal-1990)

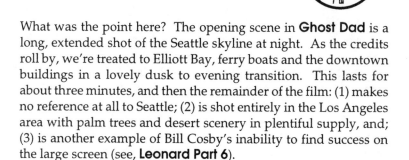

What was the point here? The opening scene in **Ghost Dad** is a long, extended shot of the Seattle skyline at night. As the credits roll by, we're treated to Elliott Bay, ferry boats and the downtown buildings in a lovely dusk to evening transition. This lasts for about three minutes, and then the remainder of the film: (1) makes no reference at all to Seattle; (2) is shot entirely in the Los Angeles area with palm trees and desert scenery in plentiful supply, and; (3) is another example of Bill Cosby's inability to find success on the large screen (see, **Leonard Part 6**).

MY OWN PRIVATE IDAHO
(Fine Line Pictures-1991)

Perhaps the finest film about young, narcoleptic, gay street hustlers from Idaho ever set in Seattle, **My Own Private Idaho** is a strange and disturbing vision from Portland's king of art cinema, Gus Van Sant. The film has some limited Seattle footage near the Pike Place Market, downtown near the Westin, and in the neighborhoods, but not enough to register a needle. Film buffs may want to check out the movie for the performance by the late River Phoenix, and for a hilarious scene in a gay porno magazine store where the coverboys come to life and converse.

THE HAND THAT ROCKS THE CRADLE
(Hollywood Pictures-1992)

As the film opens, we meet Claire Bartel (Annabella Sciorra), an oh-so-tasteful and correct yuppie, with an oh-so-sensitive husband,

and an oh-so-perfect house. What could go wrong? Plenty. Claire's is molested by her obstetrician who blows his brains out when Claire blows the whistle. Fast forward a few months, and the Bartels are in need of a nanny for their new baby. Who should appear at the doorstep but Peyton Flanders (Rebecca de Mornay), the widow of the departed doctor. Using the logic that seems peculiar to all movie psychos, Peyton has reckoned that since Claire has destroyed her family, she will repay the favor and spends the rest of the movie doing so. Despite the growing signs of trouble, the Bartel's remain oblivious to Peyton's scheming. (They must be charter members of "Densa.") In one particularly implausible sequence, she appears soaking wet in a transparent nightgown to seduce Michael. He refuses, an act which led the authors of **Bad Movies We Love** to note that he is "unmistakably the invention of a woman writer."

While **The Hand that Rocks the Cradle** contains only a moderate dose of Seattle footage (as well as some Tacoma locations), it does excel at capturing the oh-so-serene Seattle yuppie lifestyle of the late 1980's. Midway through the film there is a nice sequence in downtown Seattle near Rainier Square, and a beautiful shot down University Street toward the waterfront. Later, we take a visit to the Auditorium Cleaners in Fremont to pick-up some laundry and see the Aurora Bridge in the background. The Magnolia area is also featured as the location of the deceased doctor's home. The address of the house is 2502 37th Avenue West and it features a panoramic view back towards the city and Elliott Bay. In an authentic local touch, the house is listed for sale by Windermere Realty, which no doubt paid handsomely for the advertisement. We can just see the ad campaign now — "Molested by your obstetrician and stalked by his psychotic widow? Come see us for just the right property." There are also brief cameos by Cliff Lenz and Penny LeGate from KING-TV, and by Kimberly Hill, formerly of the Channel 11 Ten O'clock News.

TWIN PEAKS: FIRE WALK WITH ME (Columbia/Tri-Star-1992)

There's a lot to be said for David Lynch's quirky and offbeat television series Twin Peaks in promoting the state's film and video industry. Many feel that this cult favorite helped reawaken national interest in the northwest as a major film and video location, and certainly the timing of the series helped launch Seattle into national cultural prominence. Unfortunately, that still isn't enough to make Twin Peaks: Fire Walk With Me a good Seattle movie or a good movie, period. The bulk of this film (as with the television series), was shot in and around North Bend, Snoqualmie, Fall City and Everett. Even the sight of a few empty Rainier beer bottles in one bar scene cant keep this one off the "rest of " pages.

BORN TO BE WILD
Warner Brothers-1994

Originally titled "Katie," **Born to be Wild** tells the now familiar tale of a troubled teen who learns some painful lessons about responsibility and commitment by caring for a troubled animal — in this case your average African gorilla. Young Wil Horneff plays Rick Heller, the product of a broken family whose single mother (Helen Shaver) works as a university researcher in northern California. As punishment for his recent delinquent behavior, mom forces Rick to take care of her latest research subject, a likeable gorilla named Katie. Of course, Rick slowly bonds with the ape and when Katie's evil owner (Peter Boyle) takes her back to entertain his flea market customers, Rick shows mom how much he's learned about how crime doesn't pay by stealing the gorilla and a van from the university and heading for Canada. For longtime locals, the film's parallels with the life of the Puget Sound's most famous simian Ivan the Gorilla are all too obvious.

What's Seattle in **Born to be Wild** is paltry at best. Early in the flick, there's a chase scene through the Duwamish industrial area with the City Light sign clearly visible in the background. The scenes at the flea market where Katie is put on display were filmed at the Goodwill store just off Dearborn. A couple of cameos are also worth noting. Monica Hart has a bit part as a local T.V. newscaster (natch), and John Proccacino gets the juicy role of the prosecutor who puts Rick on trial for abducting Katie. The picture actually livens up considerably when Proccacino is on screen, and we can only hope he gets a bigger role in the inevitable sequel, **Born to be Wild in the Streets**.

The Final Reel

So ends our whirlwind tour of the last 30 years of Seattle, as seen through the movies. What have we learned? First, a project like this takes planning, determination, and a lightning-quick finger on the remote. Second, Hollywood filmmakers coming to Seattle have a few preconceptions that make real Seattle a little different than its celluloid image. For example:

Seattle on Film	Real Seattle
Pretty sunny.	Sunny? Must be July 21.
Traffic, what traffic?	You know Paul Brendle better than your kids.
Music is Elvis, jazz or grunge.	Not much Elvis.
Greasy dives and carnival food.	Fresh Penn Cove mussels with radicchio in a light Japanese soy paste. That or Dick's.
Blue collar workers are exclusively fishermen or steelworkers.	Can you say airplane?
Angst-ridden con artists, convicts and thieves.	Sensitive guys with ponytail.
Decaying school buildings, burned out teachers and marauding gangs.	Well o.k., one right.

Thanks for reading our book and we hope you get a chance to see some of these films. Drop us a note with your suggestions for the next edition. We'll see you in the video stores.